1—

WHAT OTHERS ARE SAYING ABOUT *LUNCHMEAT & LIFE LESSONS*

"Laced with the wisdom and insight that only comes through experience, this book beautifully exemplifies the unbreakable bond between father and daughter."

—Stephen R. Covey, author,
The 7 Habits of Highly Effective People and
The 8th Habit: From Effectiveness to Greatness

"I knew John Bichelmeyer and he lived every word of his own advice. He was a fine butcher, a loving father and a caring and committed man. An excellent tribute."

—George Brett, Kansas City Royals baseball legend
American League MVP, MLB Hall of Famer and father of three

This book is fantastic! I was really taken by the philosophies of the Butcher... I think his wisdom is very applicable at our organization. In fact, I am going to be using some of your material in my speech at our sales meeting in Colorado next week for about 500 of our people.

—David M. Lockton, Chairman
Lockton Companies

I rarely get emotional when reading a book, but this one "got" me, your book hits home. I could not help but reflect on all the little sayings and stories my role models have told me in the past. Reading the "Butcher's Wisdom" helped me realign my values, not only in my personal life but in my business career. The lessons shared, through your father's teachings, are incredibly applicable in my business and in how my associates handle client services.

—Tim Donnelly, Founder & President
SoftVu LLC

Cherished every word of your book! I LOVED it and so did my wife Cass, who read it and immediately shared it with our daughter-in-law!

—*Hyler Bracey, Author of Managing from the Heart & Building Trust: How to Get It! How to Keep It!*

It is as inspiring to me as anything I have ever read…you have provided us all such a gift with writing this. I am going to hang a summary of the "Butcher's Wisdom" in my office.

—*Denise Deans-Graf, Nursefinders COO Staffing*

What a blessing you gave me by sharing your father's wisdom. This book was a work of love, which is evident on every page. I am better for having read it.

—*Eunice Karp, Certified Life Coach Hudson Institute*

The truth is I have never read any book, poem or tribute in my life that has touched me more.

—*Melissa Moore, President & CEO Strategic Edge Solutions*

Thank you for the tears and inspiration. This book was inspiring, touching, funny and simply perfect!

—*Nancy Halverson, Vice President-Talent Development Spherion Corporation*

I just finished reading your book. My first reaction was- WOW! I thought of my mother and my grandparents and how they influenced my life with their simple but profound guidance. I must say, though, I didn't learn nearly as much from them as I did from the old country butcher!

—*Shawn Francis, Vice President- New Business Development Alloy Wheel*

This book reconfirms the simple values all businesses (and business people) need to incorporate in their daily practices.

—*Ann Phillips, Owner and President Mobilfone*

A wonderful story of life's wisdoms as shared by a simple butcher with his daughter. It is a love story, a collection of life's lessons and a guide for everyone in business on how to be truly successful.

—*Robert Morgan, Chief Operating Officer Talent Management Hudson*

Lunchmeat & Life Lessons

Sharing a Butcher's Wisdom

LUNCHMEAT & LIFE LESSONS

Sharing a Butcher's Wisdom

By Mary B. Lucas, B.D.

MBL Press

Lunchmeat & Life Lessons

Published by MBL Press
A division of MBL Consulting, LLC

For further information,
please contact the author at:

mary@consultwithmbl.com

Book design by,

Arbor Books, Inc.
www.arborbooks.com

Printed in the United States

Lunchmeat & Life Lessons: Sharing a Butcher's Wisdom
Mary B. Lucas
1. Title 2. Author 3. Biography/Inspirational/Motivational

Library of Congress Control Number: 2006909931

ISBN 10: 0-9791234-0-2
ISBN 13: 978-0-9791234-0-5

Dedication

For Mom,
because I know you loved him
every bit as much as I did,
and I know you knew
I loved you every bit as much, too!

Contents

ACKNOWLEDGMENTS

FROM THE BEGINNING, there was the support of my entire family and that has never wavered. Throughout my childhood, career and adult life, you all remained my mainstay, and still are. A special thank you goes to my siblings—Joan, Judy, Johnny, Jimmy, Joey, Jerry, Jeannie, Jane and Barbie. I love you all more than words can tell.

To my "boys", Scott, Chase and Nick, I thank you for being my greatest fans as I am eternally yours. How blessed we are to have each other!

As Dad would say, "You gotta dance with the ones that brung ya." And with that in mind, I thank Ray Marcy and Gary Peck who started with me in the "people business" and have stayed a constant in my life since the day we met so early in my career.

To those of you who have touched my life as you have come in and out of it, I thank you for being such an incredible part of my story. I would not have been able to write this book without you. I always have and always will send you my warmest regards.

To the "Goddesses" from the Hudson Institute who inspired me to begin this journey, to Tina Aulita, Andrea Sumpter, Luke Wetzel and Betsy Donnelly who helped me along the way, and to Hyler Bracey and Lou Savary without whom there wouldn't be the book you hold in your hands today, my gratitude is overwhelming.

Last, yes, but never least, to my baby sister Dr. Barbara Bichelmeyer and my "satellite sisters" Gayle Selby, Dee Dee Deans-Graf and Lesa Francis, thank you for your final edits, additions and encouragement to move forward.

You ALL have inspired me!

FOREWORD

ALTHOUGH I AM PROUD OF MY BACHELOR'S DEGREE and will forever be loyal to my Alma Mater, ultimately, nothing can compare to the letters of distinction my father bestowed upon me: my "B.D." degree, which stands for "Butcher's Daughter."

I earned my B.D. by spending hours seated across the butcher-block table in my mother's kitchen—my classroom—listening to my father's lessons about how to deal with life's beginnings and endings and all the ups and downs in between. All were lessons I could apply to my own life, wisdom that helped me to be a successful executive as well as a more loving and committed wife and mother.

Nearly 25 years have passed since I was hired for my first "real" job as a staffing coordinator at a temporary help service. I found myself working in the ultimate "people business" and I really loved that it was so simple to explain what I did: I helped people find the work they wanted and companies find the people they wanted.

It was during this time that I got my first lessons in Butcher's Wisdom from my father. When, I left to start my own consulting company, I was still at the top of my game in the people business, making more money than I ever had imagined I would make and having just earned another promotion. I had become one of the top executives in a staffing company with annual revenues of more than $2 billion. And even in the midst of enormous change and many leaders at my level coming and going through the executive revolving door, I had "made it."

I credit my B.D. degree as the number one reason I flourished in the people business and continue to thrive in an industry where many quickly grow tired of "people." I made it by keeping myself motivated and, in turn, motivating others.

However, when you work in an industry that is solely reliant on people as their product, you have to work at getting re-inspired and re-motivated on a regular basis. Like many other executives, I drew from Stephen Covey and his book, *The Seven Habits of Highly Effective People,* and I revered the secrets Hyler Bracey reveals in his book, *Managing from the Heart.*

Oddly enough, I also found great support on difficult days from the simplicity of the messages in two children's books: *Move on Frog* and *Lily's Purple Plastic Purse.*

But more than anywhere else, I drew inspiration from my most cherished source, the lessons I learned from the time spent with my father.

CHAPTER ONE:

In the Beginning

THIS STORY STARTS ON A WEDNESDAY MORNING in May of 1980, three days after I graduated from college. I had earned a B.S. in Journalism and Mass Communications from Kansas State University. Like my sisters before me, I planned only to work temporarily until I was married and had children. However, my life didn't turn out that way.

The day after I graduated from K-State, I had come back home to live at my parents' house while I looked for a job. That first day home, Monday, full of enthusiasm, I had walked into a temporary help office to see if they could place me for the summer, until I could find a "real job" at an advertising agency.

I filled out an application at this temporary employment agency hoping they could find me a job somewhere. Instead, when they read my qualifications and interviewed me, they asked if I would like to work for them, right there in their office helping other applicants find jobs throughout the city.

My "yes" was immediate.

I was told to wait for their call telling me whether or not I had the job.

Two days later, Wednesday, I was lounging out in the late-morning sun on our second-floor deck in a bathing suit, my body slathered in iodine and baby oil—It may sound crazy, but that's what people my age in Kansas did back then—when my Dad called upstairs to tell me I had a phone call.

It was the call I'd been waiting for.

After I hung up, I came running into the kitchen, still in my bathing suit with a towel wrapped around me, my lanky self all arms and legs, waving my hands and shouting, "I got the job! I got the job!"

"You got the job! That's great!" my Dad said proudly, with a big wrinkly smile. He stood up and opened his arms to give me a congratulatory hug, ignoring the fact that I was covered in oil.

He had been seated at his favorite place in our kitchen, at the butcher-block table, with a cup of coffee steaming alongside his plate of bacon, eggs and fried potatoes. There was the proverbial plate of sliced salami waiting in the middle of the table.

Everyone's favorite place to talk was really an "island" in the middle of the kitchen, made of butcher-block wood, where four or five of us could easily get together. It was a bar-height table my Dad got from the butcher supply warehouse. He had a wrap-around counter made for it so we could sit on barstools around it. It was *the* gathering place for our family and for anyone who came over to the house to visit—other family and friends as well as Dad's employees and customers.

At the time, Dad was 64 years old with a lumbering build, a big man in every way. In his earlier years, he claimed he was always a little over six feet tall, but as his back bowed with age he stood just a little taller than I was at that time, and I am five-ten. He was not overweight, but he really was larger than life. As I was so skinny at that age, he was probably three times as wide as I was.

"Is this the job you applied for on Monday," he asked, "the one where you work with people?"

"Yes, that's the one." I didn't have the heart to remind him that it was the only job I'd interviewed for, so far. When you're one of ten children, your parents need reminders from time to time to help them keep up with the goings on in your life.

You see, I was born the ninth of ten children to John and Mary Bichelmeyer of Shawnee, Kansas. Unlike my eight siblings before me, Joan, Judy, Johnny, Jimmy, Joey, Jerry, Jeannie and Jane, I was the first child whose name didn't start with a "J." Because my parents thought that I would be the last baby they would bring in to this world (my mother was 40 at the time), my father insisted that I be named Mary after my mother. Two years later, my baby sister Barbie came along and surprised everybody!

Here I was in our kitchen, all grown up, I thought, having my first adult-to-adult conversation with my father standing in front of him, barefoot and wrapped in a towel, the rest of my body covered in oil.

"And you'll work in an office?" he asked, looking up at me with a question mark in his wide, brown eyes and in his voice.

"Yes, in an office." I replied proudly, hands on my hips, emphasizing the word "office."

I have to preface this situation by saying that this was an unusual set of circumstances for my father to find himself in. My brothers were butchers and most of my sisters had been employed as teachers before becoming full-time moms. I was the first to break that trend. I was pretty pleased with myself (in truth, maybe a little too pleased) to be the first child to get a job in an office.

"Well, sit down," he said. "I think we need to have a chat."

He motioned to the other side of the butcher block for me to have a seat.

"So," he said, "you're going into the business world."

"Yes, Dad," I nodded, as I pulled a stool up to the table and sat down. "I am."

"And you're going to work in an office?" He shook his head and looked up at one of the beams in the ceiling, as if this fact was somehow bewildering to him, as if he wasn't sure what advice to give to a child of his who would work in an office.

Such a response from my father was not unusual as our family history had always been more blue collar than white. We were all raised on a farm in the Kansas City area by two of the most generous, loving and wise parents. My father, a country boy who came from a family of ten children, began working in the stockyards, and then made his living as a butcher. He married my mother, a city girl who was an only child and whose passion was taking care of her family.

I grinned at him and said, with even more emphasis, "Yes, an office."

"What kind of office?" he said.

"It's an office where we help people find temporary jobs," I said.

"What kinds of jobs?"

"I'm not completely sure, Dad, but I think some office workers like secretaries, typists and stenographers, and I do know that they also do a lot of placement they call 'light industrial.' I think that means warehouse workers, you know, loading and unloading trucks. Things like that."

"Why would they come to you and not look in the newspaper for jobs?"

"We have a list of companies who need people, and we find people to fill those needs, they work for us."

"Why would companies go through you instead of hiring their own people?"

"We save the companies time they would spend interviewing dozens of applicants. Instead, we send the person with the right qualifications directly there, ready to start work that morning."

"Well," he thought for a moment. "I'm not sure what the heck to tell you because I've never worked in an office—nothing like that."

I simply said, "That's okay."

I reached for a slice of salami and wrapped it in a piece of white bread.

"But I can tell you what made me successful in business," he offered. "You're going into the people business, right?"

"Yes, Dad." I sat there patiently, munching on my salami.

"Well, let me tell you what I think is the key to being successful in the people business."

"Okay."

"You need to show 'em what you're made of," he said resolutely, pointing his fork at me.

"Okay." I have to admit that at this point I was humoring him. I leaned over the table, smiled, looked him in the eye and repeated, "Show 'em what you're made of."

He nodded.

BUTCHER'S WISDOM

Show 'em what you're made of!

"You know, back when I first opened the meat market I used to tell my new employees that you have to remember when someone walks in this door to 'show 'em what you're made of.' And the best way to do that is by remembering that the first hunk of meat you sell is yourself."

I all but laughed at him.

"Dad, are you sure that's what you want to be advising your daughter as she goes out into the business world?"

"Yes, I am certain that's the first thing I'd tell you and that is why I am telling you now," he assured me.

"Is that what you did, Dad?"

"Yes, so let me explain it to you," he said, only slightly less patiently. "When I left the stockyards to open the meat market I was worried sick that I wasn't going to be able to make it out on my own. It was scary because I wouldn't be getting a steady paycheck anymore."

"That was very brave, Dad."

He walked over to the stove to refill his cup with hot water, a spoonful of instant coffee and three spoonfuls of sugar.

"Nothing was certain except that I had six mouths to feed at the time and that it was my money that I was spending to get the business off the ground. It was a scary time for me. And I hadn't even been in business a week, when I heard that my competitors had worked out a plan to put me out of business!"

"How did you know that, Dad?"

"One of the guys I used to work with told me about a plan he had overheard my competitors discussing. Any price that I advertised, they were going to under sell me by five- or ten-cents a pound, whatever it took. They figured I'd be out of business in a month or two."

"So what happened?" I asked, at this point growing more interested in his story. My hand reached over for another slice of salami.

"Well, I'm still in business and doing very well, as you know. I proved them wrong because the thing they didn't count on was that I had so little money I *couldn't* advertise." With a satisfied grin on his face, he added, "I had invested everything we had into getting the business going, and there wasn't anything left to spend on advertising."

I laughed out loud.

And so did he.

John Bichelmeyer, my father, was a happy man. He was all about "enjoying the ride" and making the most out of what life dealt him. He was the most balanced person I have ever known. He handled the highs and lows he encountered in a way that inspired me and others, and he would often remind those around him that they "shouldn't take life too seriously because they were never going to get out of it alive anyway!"

"So, what did you do to compete?" I asked.

"I got all of my employees together and I told them what I wanted from them. I expected them to greet every customer as soon as they walked in the door by looking them in the eye and giving them a smile. If we were busy and customers had to take a number, I expected them to keep checking on everyone: 'How you doing, Number 14? You still with me, Number ten?' We were going to get to know their names and who they were and what they did. I told them to always remember that 'the first hunk of meat you sell is yourself!'"

As my Dad told me his story, it was becoming increasingly more obvious that he might know a little something about the people business.

I have to admit I was impressed. Maybe his message wasn't very sophisticated, but even before I started work the next day I found myself thinking often of the advice he gave me and hoping to find opportunities to apply his principle.

Even now, I can recall opening the office door on my first day of work as a staffing coordinator. Getting dressed, I had lots of coaching from my mother and sisters on what I should wear. I finally settled on a simple white blouse, a navy skirt, and flat shoes. I knew that, even in stocking feet, I would be a head taller than any other woman I had seen there on

Monday. I debated whether to wear my hair up or to let it hang over my shoulders. I decided to let it hang.

I walked into the office remembering my father's advice, to 'show 'em what you're made of.' But as soon as I opened the door and looked around, I realized that none of the applicants could ever see what I was made of. They couldn't see anything of anyone.

What applicants saw when they came in was a solid wall with a solid door. Over on the side, almost chest high, was a sliding glass window. When their presence was known, an arm reached out and handed them an application form to fill out. So, for the first ten or fifteen minutes, applicants never saw who was behind that solid wall. They got to come behind the door only when we interviewed them. But for those first minutes, they couldn't tell whether we were happy to see them, or whether we even cared one way or another.

In contrast, I was so aware that at my Dad's butcher shop, the moment a customer came through the door, my father or one of the staff would greet her with a smile and a hearty hello, as though the shop had been waiting just for her and, now that she had arrived, she was making their day. From that first moment, everyone in that butcher shop was showing what they were made of.

I realized that none of that was happening here in my office. However, I was the new employee, and was taking orders from the ones behind the wall. "I can at least show *them* what I am made of," I thought to myself.

I paid attention and was a quick learner, and by noon I had caught onto the system, but I was still feeling sorry for the applicants on the other side of the wall who didn't get to see a smiling face for at least ten minutes.

My desk was located right behind the big door. I, too, was just looking at a closed door and a wall.

After lunch, I asked if anyone would mind if I opened the door. Nobody objected, so I opened the door all the way and positioned my desk so that the moment someone walked in the office, they wouldn't be looking at a closed door or a solid wall, but at me. And I would be smiling. I would greet them and make them feel welcomed and wanted. I would walk out from behind my desk, shake their hand and personally hand them an application form. I would assure them that I would be happy to help if they had any questions.

As I was meeting people, I would always ask myself: "Did I show 'em what I was made of? Did I make a good first impression? Did I sell myself?"

I had a feeling that my Dad would be proud of his daughter. She was showing them what she had, even on her first day.

In most small to mid-size businesses, showing what you're made of is still as simple as answering the phone by the third ring every time with a "Thank you for calling." It's as simple as not saying, "Please Hold," immediately when someone calls without greeting them. It's as simple as welcoming people the moment they walk in the door by looking up at them and smiling and saying, "So happy you are here" and "I have been looking forward to meeting you"—and really meaning it!

In larger companies, I think it's more of a challenge these days to find a way to get back to making customers feel like they are more important than the big business concern of "lowering transaction costs," especially when cost-cutting is done at the expense of good old-fashioned customer service.

Perhaps all companies should learn a lesson from the Butcher's Wisdom and worry less about their advertising budget and more about how they can best begin every interaction by "selling themselves."

BUTCHER'S WISDOM

The first hunk of meat
you sell is yourself!

CHAPTER TWO:

Create a Lasting Impression

DAD WAS ALWAYS SOMEWHAT LARGER THAN LIFE and I don't think I would say I was particularly close to him when I was younger. He was the "fun Dad" with my school friends, making up rhymes with their names and telling stories that would make them laugh. Don't get me wrong—I was proud of him and I loved him, but in my teen years I never sought out his opinion or even asked his advice about anything.

To be honest, I'm not sure I really valued his opinions, that is, until the day I got my first real job and we had our first real adult conversation across the butcher-block table. That's when it all really began. It was the day he told me to "Show 'em what you're made of."

Well-known in his community as the "city philosopher," my father was a man with only an eighth-grade education. Married at the height of the Great Depression, he worked three jobs to support our growing family and still managed to save enough money to fulfill his dream of owning and operating his own butcher shop. Nearly 60 years later, Bichelmeyer Meat Company remains a successful business that is still family owned and operated.

In that first adult conversation at the butcher block, still talking about my new job, my Dad gave me a second important piece of advice. "And the next thing I'm going to tell you," he said, "is that you need to always remember to put the 'comeback sauce' on every person you come in contact with."

I burst out laughing. "Dad, I'm pretty sure you don't want me out in the work world offering people 'comeback sauce.'"

"Of course I do. I told everyone that worked for me exactly what I just told you. 'Don't ever forget to put on the comeback sauce.' If they ask for a pound of lunchmeat, you give them a few more slices and smile and tell them you gave them a little bit more—whatever it takes to connect with people. Whenever they walk out the door, ask yourself if you think that they left happy. Always remember the comeback sauce and feel free to do whatever you need to do to make sure they leave with the feeling that they want to come back again soon."

He nodded at me and continued. "It's really about getting people from the get-go and doing everything you can to make sure they don't ever want to let go."

"Right from the get-go," I repeated.

He looked at me with seriousness, "I'm pretty sure those things apply to what you're going to be doing. I'm a butcher. You're an office worker. We're both in the people business."

I wasn't sure about that connection at that moment, but I soon realized the truth of my Dad's insight.

Did I remember the 'comeback sauce' the next day at work?

During the first few days, my comeback sauce was pretty basic. I smiled a lot. I noticed things about the person that impressed me and that I could comment on. "You have a wonderful smile." "You are certainly having a great hair day today." Things like that.

As I got better and better at it, I learned to close each first interview with a prospective employee by setting expectations of what was likely to happen next. That specific moment in the interview, when nothing yet was certain about their being placed, was a great opportunity for adding some comeback sauce.

For one thing, I had to make sure they would come back to us, and not run off to some other job placement agency if I did not have an assignment for them right away.

In the temporary help business, I found out that I needed to use two different brands of comeback sauce, one for the people that we were certain to build a working relationship with, the other for those we were not likely to put on assignment.

In the people business, everyone you interact with deserves at least some type of comeback sauce.

To the first brand of comeback sauce I gave the unwieldy name: "I want to work with you and I am pretty darn sure I will find you work, if not today then right away, so don't go applying anywhere else" brand.

Near the end of the first interview with a high potential prospective employee, I might say any or all of the following:

"I am so thrilled you came in to apply with us today. You are exactly the type of employee we want to place with our clients, and I can't wait to get you started."

If I thought I could land him or her a job on the spot, I might say something like, "If you will stick with me for a few minutes, I am going to make a couple of calls on your behalf to some of our best clients to see if we can get you started right away."

I would then wait for a nod of approval or, better still, an eager "yes."

I might then say, "To be honest, I am making these calls right now for two reasons. One, to get you placed as soon as possible and, two, to show you the kind of commitment we make to our employees. We will work for you as your career agent."

If I got another nod or a yes, I might say, "Now, I know you have other staffing companies you can apply with, but I am hoping that by showing you the kind of commitment we make, you will allow me the opportunity to place you on at least one assignment before you go anywhere else. Deal?"

If I got the nod again, I would make those calls to the most likely employers.

With comeback sauce like that, we usually not only kept these employees on our payroll, but we also got others who came to us on their recommendation.

Comeback sauce quickly became the best free advertising we ever got.

The second brand of comeback sauce was based on my Dad's constant reminder that honesty is the best policy. Though I can't claim that wise statement to originate from him, I did observe him as he applied it in his own life.

I found it to be especially important in my new role *not* to lead people on, if I knew after an interview that I would not be able to use someone in our particular staffing office. I felt obligated to be upfront and let them know.

For people like that, I used a special brand of comeback sauce. I called it the "I don't think your skills are an exact match for the openings we typically get, but I assure you if the situation changes we will let you know" brand.

Here's what a typical encounter sounded like:

"I am so grateful that you took the time to come meet with me today. I am very sorry to tell you this, but at this time I don't think your skills are a match for the openings we typically get here. I promise you, if that situation changes, we will let you know."

That is a polite way of saying "no," but it does not yet qualify as comeback sauce. You have to go a bit further. You have to do what you can do to help such a person find a job or get some reward for coming.

You might say, "In the meantime, after studying your qualifications, why don't you try So-and-So or So-and-So *[I would give them specific names, addresses and phone numbers of other staffing companies in the city]* to see if they have something that may be the right fit for you."

I might even agree to place a call to someone I knew at one or another of these staffing companies, if the applicant wanted.

I would always end, "And please remember, if you know of anyone else who does have the office skills we are looking for, send them our way. Tell them to mention your name when they come to us, and we will send a referral bonus your way!"

You really want to make sure everybody leaves you feeling good about the interaction they just had with you. Sometimes that may only require a simple "thank you." Best case, hopefully, they will tell others about their positive experience with you.

As I look back now at how comeback sauce works, I really think it is also a kind of insurance policy, because if you don't use it, if they leave *not* feeling good about you, statistics say they will tell a lot more people about a bad experience than they will a good one. It's just human nature that people like to talk about the bad stuff more than the good. In the people business, you never know who the applicant's mother or father, aunt or uncle, brother or sister, boyfriend or girlfriend might be. One of their relatives or friends could be a buyer of your services, your best account or your biggest prospect. That person could be the one who signs your paycheck.

I personally think comeback sauce is the key to referrals in any business, especially the people business.

The thing about comeback sauce that my Dad really impressed upon me was that everybody ought to get a little, whether you want to see them again or not. You want every person you interact with to leave impressed that you are the kind of person they would like to interact with again, even if this particular meeting did not result in an outcome one of you may have wanted.

Chances are some day, somewhere, your paths will cross again and the legacy you leave them with and how they feel about you can be altered dramatically if you remembered the comeback sauce during your last encounter.

Years went by, and as I moved up the corporate ladder, I would hear in more professional and academic language the same principles my father shared with me the morning he advised me how to approach my new role. Maybe it's me, but slogans like "You never get a second chance to make a first impression" or "Take every chance you get to make a lasting impression" never hit home for me the way "The first hunk of meat you sell is yourself" or "Don't forget the comeback sauce" did. Those were the principles I worked on implementing every day of my personal and professional life, when I remembered to be my best self.

You see, after every one of our talks I would leave that table feeling loved, valued and a little wiser and more prepared to pursue my dreams by following his guiding principles—principles that first and foremost helped to motivate me and that in turn helped me to motivate others.

BUTCHER'S WISDOM

Remember the comeback sauce

Chapter Three:

Stay Focused

AT WORK, IT REALLY WASN'T COMPLICATED to start "showing 'em what I was made of" and "putting on the comeback sauce." As long as things were going smoothly, it was easy to follow Dad's simple guidelines. The hardest part was remembering to practice these principles when things got tough and I got distracted.

Several months into my first job, things were going pretty well. However, I started to realize that other people around me could easily affect whether I had a good day or a bad day, based on how their days were going.

In truth, there were a lot of things that went on around me that could easily distract me from my work when I let them—things that at times really brought me down. There was always a lot of office drama. For example, one individual in particular would often make it difficult for me to focus on my work. She would do it by drawing me into the folds of her personal life or by talking about all "the sins" of our boss. Being new to the business world, I didn't know for certain what behavior was normal and what wasn't. I only knew what felt right to me personally. After a few months, I went back to my Dad and asked for more advice.

We were at the butcher-block table having tea and coffee, and my father asked me, "How are things going?"

"Well, I think I'm doing a good job connecting with people the way you described. And I know I'm doing a good job putting on the comeback sauce because they're coming back."

"That's good," he said.

"But the thing that's not fun," I confided, "is when I find myself getting caught up in the negatives around me. I am really not very proud of this, Dad, but sometimes I get distracted because I get to talking with my co-workers about personal problems, or we start going on and on about something negative about our boss or a client or one of our temporaries. And when I do this it really does get me down."

"That's no surprise," he said. "For some reason, most people get more of a kick out of pointing out what is wrong than they do acknowledging what is right. You will be much happier if you can focus on the good, because thinking negative makes work a lot less fun."

I nodded in agreement.

"But, Dad, it's pretty easy to get caught up in all of it. Frankly, I work with some people that spend a lot of time focusing on the negative and aren't very happy, and it's starting to make *me* unhappy."

Once again, I was hoping my Dad would have some wisdom on how to stay focused.

"All right," he thought for a moment, "I think it is time to tell you about the blinders."

"The blinders?" I asked.

"When you find yourself getting distracted, getting caught up in the negatives and you are feeling uneasy about a conversation you are having," he said, "you have to start reminding yourself to get out your blinders and put them on."

"Dad, what in the world does that mean?"

"Let me explain it to you by telling you what I did when

one of my employees started getting all caught-up in everybody else's business but his own."

I took a sip of my tea and waited for his story.

"I had been in business for a while," he began, "and I had been really lucky with the people I had hired. Everyone seemed to get along well until I brought in a fellow named Hank. After a while, I noticed that things were just not feeling right at the market anymore. There seemed to be a lot of side conversations going on all over the place, and a few of my most devoted employees started confiding in me that there were 'some people' getting pretty unhappy with me and the way I was running things."

"Oh-oh!" I said sympathetically.

"I wasn't blind to this and I pretty much gathered that the 'some people' started with Hank. I knew he was a strong-willed guy and a bit full of himself, but he was a hard worker and I appreciated what he did for the market. Still, I knew I had to talk to him, because it was obvious that he was nosing around in everyone else's business and second-guessing everything I was doing. Because of the way he shared his concerns with everyone, I could feel other employees starting to second-guess me too."

"So, what did you do?"

"One afternoon I asked Hank to take a walk with me across the street to The Bar-b-que so I could talk to him. We sat down and I started our conversation by telling him that I grew up on a farm and about a time I remembered asking my Dad why he put blinders on the horses' eyes. My Dad told me that it was because he wanted them focused on moving forward, not distracted by what was happening to their left or to their right."

"And then Hank said, 'Thanks for the history lesson, John, but I am not sure what that has to do with me.'

"I told him, 'Hank, there's some stuff going on around here and I don't like what I'm hearing. Everyone's getting all distracted at the butcher shop by stuff that has nothing to do with the business. Now, I have a favor to ask of you. I would really appreciate it if you would put on *your* blinders a little more often.'"

"'Put my blinders on?' Hank was puzzled.

"'Yes, put your blinders on. If you've got a problem with me, Hank, I'd really appreciate it if you'd come talk to *me* about it. I'm making the best decisions I know how to make and if you think that there's a problem, I'd appreciate you telling me because maybe you've got some ideas that would help me. But you're not helping me by talking about me to everybody else, getting everybody second-guessing what I'm doing here. I guess you could say that I'm going to ask that, as long as you are working here, you put your blinders on and keep 'em on.'"

The concept of "putting on your blinders" and hearing the story about how my father handled the situation with Hank really helped me throughout my career. By not getting angry or defensive, but instead asking for Hank's help in rectifying the situation, my father put his own principles in action.

Once again, I learned something from a man who I wasn't so sure initially could teach me anything about surviving and thriving in the work world. The blinders principle was a good reminder for me to focus on what was most important, and it also helped others to perceive me as a "doer" rather than someone who would allow herself to get all caught up in office drama.

I know I was young and new to the business world when I started work, but Samantha, my Branch Manager, who wasn't that much older than I was, made up for my naiveté. She was far more experienced than I was in many ways.

Before she came to work in the staffing industry and was hired to be the manager and lead salesperson for our office, she had enjoyed a successful career selling advertising for a local newspaper. She was a character, very fun-loving and quite the party girl!

This spontaneous quality really bothered Lily, one of the women I worked with who was my peer. Lily was the mother of three almost-grown children and, when I met her, she was very involved with planning her daughter's wedding. In fact, every free moment she had she invested in planning that wedding. All the while she planned, she thanked her lucky stars—and informed all of us—that her daughter was nothing like Sam.

The three of us looked like we came from three different planets. Sam was short and voluptuous, but still very rough around the edges. Her hair hung long, wavy, thick and black and her eyes were always lined in black and smudged to a sort of "smoldering look" that would have been more appropriate at a night club, according to Lily, and not at our office.

In contrast, Lily had that plastic go-to-the-beauty-shop-once-a week-for-styling hair, and she always wore blue frosty eye shadow. Her entire look might have been considered about 10 years behind the times.

I remember each of them so well because they were just so different from me at the time. I was the fresh-faced, bean-pole farm girl who never wore make up except when I was given samples that Sam or Lily didn't want after they went to the Lancôme or Clinique cosmetic counters during department store "Special Gift" days.

Proper Lily did not agree with how Sam conducted herself during her "off" hours and sometimes during her "on" hours. She did not hesitate to share her concerns about the "Sam" topic, as often as I would allow my blinders to come off and engage in a round of "Sam bashing."

The way I tried to handle it was to deflect a Sam put-down by responding with a comment about something that was good about her. I have to admit that at times it was hard to do, because I often felt the same way Lily did.

When I defended Sam, Lily would laugh at me, calling me a "Pollyanna." There was some truth to her claim, because if I wanted to be my best self I would have to be a bit Pollyanna, pointing out what was good about Sam.

But the real reason I did it was to keep my blinders on.

It wasn't that hard to do because, deep down, I could find things I liked and admired about Sam. She was very different from anyone I had ever known, totally uninhibited in many ways. I found myself saying things like, "You gotta love her, don't you?" or "That's our Sam!" in order to avoid getting caught up supporting the jabs Lily would throw at her.

I tried to point out to Lily that the fact that Sam was so uninhibited was the very reason she was fearless in sales. It was a quality that could and did serve her well personally. It also helped our office rankings. We were by then one of the top 20 company offices in the country. We had to admit our sales kept growing primarily because of her.

Don't get me wrong—my blinders fell off often, and at times they still do. In fact, of all the principles my Dad taught me, this is the one I have the hardest time following at work and at home. But when I really live this principle, it is the one that brings me the most respect.

Early in my career, I am certain that it was because I managed to keep my blinders on the majority of the time that I was able to earn the deep respect of my boss and coworkers. This principle was the career compass I used that ultimately kept me facing in the right direction at work—forward!

Years later, I had the opportunity to hear Stephen Covey, the author of the book *The Seven Habits of Highly Effective*

People speak about this same concept. When he spoke of the importance of staying in your "circle of influence" (concentrating on things you can control) and not spending too much time in the "circle of concern" (worrying and gossiping about things you have no control over), I had to smile. Here was Dr. Stephen Covey, the well-respected and highly educated author and teacher, sharing with an audience of hundreds the same basic principle my father taught me, face-to-face, across the butcher-block table, when he said, "I think it is time to tell you about the blinders."

BUTCHER'S WISDOM

Get out your blinders and put them on.

CHAPTER FOUR:

Make Something Happen

EVERY ONCE IN A WHILE I THINK OF AN EVENT that is "so Dad," as my siblings and I would say. One such event I call "The Lunch Date" or "You can take the boy out of the country, but you can't take the country out of the boy."

About five months after I started working, Dad asked me if he could come down to my office on his way to the "hide-house" and take me to lunch. The hide-house was the drop-off point for the animal hides he salvaged each week at the butcher shop. He would haul them in the back of his pickup truck.

Even though I was thrilled to have him see me in my office, I was also a little ambivalent.

To set the stage, I need to tell you that our office was in one of the swankiest parts of Kansas City—the Country Club Plaza. We were upstairs from a five-star restaurant where the Kansas City elite dined and across the street from the premier department store where they shopped. Although the farm I grew up on was less than 20 miles away from my office, given the differences in styles of living, it may as well have been in another galaxy.

I have to admit that I felt the need to prepare everyone in my office for Dad's visit, saying that I wasn't sure what he would show up wearing, knowing that he would be on his way to the hide-house. I even went as far as to ask Dad to dress appropriately for my swanky office, but I still wasn't sure what clothes he would show up in.

He arrived at my office to take me to lunch and I've never been so proud. He was perfect. He was wearing a crisp white shirt, bolo tie, a straw hat and he smelled wonderful. I introduced him to Sam and Lily, and then we walked to a German deli just down the way.

It was a hot but beautiful Indian summer day and I couldn't have been more proud to be on his arm as we walked down the street. It was the perfect father-daughter moment.

We walked into the deli and I felt even more proud when all of the men behind the counter were greeting him by name because they were all customers of his butcher shop. As he made conversation with everyone, asking how business was going or talking about the sausage they were selling, I really got to see his principles in action.

After we sat down to eat, Dad congratulated me on my job.

"So, you're really doing well?" he asked.

"Yes, Dad. I really am. I think they're really happy with me," I nodded. "I'm having fun and I can't believe that they pay me to do this! Don't get me wrong. It's not perfect. I run into problems all the time, things I am not that comfortable with."

"Like what?" he asked.

"Like firing people. That is never fun," I replied. "There's this one guy whose grandmother has died so many times I finally asked him how many grandmothers he had, because it seemed like he could never make it to work because he was always going to a funeral. I eventually had to let him go, but even that guy thanked me for how I handled it—for being up-front with him. And it's all because I never forget the comeback sauce, even when I have to deliver bad news."

"So, tell me the story," he said, leaning closer to me, "of how you did it."

He was eager to hear my tale.

I told him about this light industrial employee I worked with named Jerome. I had placed Jerome on several assignments and he was a good worker when he went to work, but he had a little trouble being as consistent in appearing on the job as he needed to be. He would call me early in the morning saying he could not go to work that day because his "grandmother had died." After giving me the same excuse several times, I pretty much figured this was his standard "get out of work" story. But I never accused him of lying. I always thanked him for calling to let me know, and I always told him that I was very sorry for his loss, until it got to the point where his not going to work just wasn't going to work for us anymore. It really didn't matter why he wasn't going to work, it just mattered that he was consistently not showing up and that I could not count on him.

The last time he called to say that he couldn't go to work, even before he started to tell me his reason why, I said, "Jerome, you obviously have a lot going on right now in your life keeping you from work. I want you to know that I really appreciate the fact that you always call us to tell us you are not available. But the bottom line is that lately you have not been available more often than you have been. I think it is time for you to look for employment options where you might have a little more flexibility than I can offer you here. I really need you to be at work when I schedule you for it, and lately you haven't been. I do hope that your family makes it through this difficult time, and I wish you all the best finding work elsewhere when you think you are ready to make a commitment to a job that you can keep."

I will never forget his response. He said, "You knew I was lying all along and you never called me on it and you are not going to now, are you?"

We both laughed and I said, "Jerome, I did not want to question you about something that personal, but I was beginning to wonder how many grandmothers you had. I thought my family was big but yours—wow!"

We both chuckled again.

Again, I wished him well and, even though I did not really want him to come back to work for us, I made sure he got a dose of comeback sauce, because he had been a good worker for us when he was committed and I appreciated that. But most of all I appreciated all the potential referrals he could give me.

"You can never go wrong with comeback sauce," my Dad said, smiling.

"I agree, Dad. It sure has helped me so far, and you know what? I think some more good things may be coming my way." I was feeling very optimistic about work and as usual being with Dad made me feel even better.

"That's great," he smiled. "But be careful. Remember those blinders. Don't always be thinking about what's around the bend or you won't do justice to the job you have in front of you," he said.

I nodded, and he went on.

"Don't always be waving your hand, hoping to get attention all the time for what you are paid to be doing anyway. I know that, for me at the meat market, the person that always got my respect wasn't the one waving his hand in the air, begging for more money and more recognition. Instead, I took notice of the guy who had his nose to the grindstone, working so hard that he didn't have time to be a waver. If he was busy doing well with the responsibility I had already given him, chances are, when I gave him more responsibility, he'd do that well too."

"We have our share of attention-getters and wavers in our office, too," I said.

BUTCHER'S WISDOM

Don't be a waver—Do be a doer.

"I don't know if you've ever heard this one," Dad said. "Truth be told, I don't remember where I heard it, but they say there are three kinds of people: those who want something to happen, those who make something happen and those who wonder what the hell happened!"

I laughed. "I've never heard that one, Dad."

"You need to decide which type of person you want to be, but it sounds to me like you're on your way to being a person who makes something happen—the kind of person who keeps her blinders on and keeps busy doing her work—and I'm proud of you."

He looked up at the clock. "Look at the time! Do you have an hour for lunch?"

"Dad," I smiled. "They know that I'm having lunch with you. My boss Sam expects that I'll be gone a little longer today, and she is fine with it."

Always the teacher, he said, "Well, you should get back on time, and set a good example of being on time all the time," he said.

BUTCHER'S WISDOM

Be on time all the time.

Then, he added in a whisper, "Besides, I've got my truck parked in front of that fancy department store across the street, and I've got a mile-high pile of hides in the back that I need to deliver. And, as hot as it is today, I am pretty sure it's starting to stink to high heaven right about now!"

On that note, we walked back out into the fancy world I was now working in, laughing.

As enamored as I was with my new surroundings, and as appalled as I was that my father's truck was most certainly causing "a stink" on the street, I had never been more proud than I was at that moment to be the "Butcher's Daughter."

BUTCHER'S WISDOM

Be a person who makes something happen.

CHAPTER FIVE:

Bring Out the Best

THREE YEARS INTO MY CAREER, I became the branch manager of the Kansas City office. As I mentioned, our office had struggled through some heavy drama during those three years when Samantha was the manager and Lily used every chance to knock her down. When Sam did not return from maternity leave, I guess because I stayed the course, she suggested that I be the one to step up to run the office in her place.

I did and, in spite of the emotional storms and everything else that had gone on, we kept growing.

By this time Lily had retired, and I was working with a small team I had hired myself. Even though there were only a few of us running things, we were a very efficient office crew. Truly, it was a phenomenal time in my career. We were consistently hitting on all cylinders. We continued to grow and month after month we ranked as one of the top three branches in the country.

Despite our continued success, I must admit that at times it was hard *not* to grow weary of working with people. It wasn't just the resistance, demands, and silly complaints of the applicants wanting work, or the clients I was placing them with. That was to be expected. What was becoming increasingly more difficult was keeping up our office momentum, keeping our little team motivated.

As the office manager, it was up to me to set an energetic and upbeat example. That was really hard when I was allowing overly demanding clients to get to me. Case in point. Our number one client at the time was a woman whom I'll call "Lisa Gray." When I say that Lisa was our number one client, I mean she was our *number one* client. Her business was the primary reason our office was consistently on top.

Lisa ran the clerical end of a big department store downtown and was a million-dollar-a-year client, which was a lot of money in those days. She hired easily three times as many workers from us as any of our other clients. And she was an absolute "you-know-what" to us. She was both demanding and condescending. Besides, she knew that she was our biggest client. It was becoming increasingly more difficult to deal with her, let alone pour on the comeback sauce, especially since almost every phone call ended in her slamming down the receiver after berating us.

The worst thing about this situation was that I was letting people see that it was bothering me. One Monday afternoon, after Lisa and I had concluded a particularly unpleasant phone call, I left the office and drove out to my parents' house. My Dad had always taken Mondays off and I desperately needed his advice.

"Dad," I sighed, as I sat down at the butcher-block table, "I'm so tired of this. I thought that after the weekend I'd be able to handle it, but I'm just overwhelmed working with this Lisa Gray."

He sat down across from me. "Now, let me get the picture straight. This woman is your biggest client, right?"

"Yes," I nodded.

"A lot bigger than your other clients? You don't have anyone that could replace her?"

"No," I thought about it for a moment. "Well, at least not right away."

"Well, the first thing I'd tell you is that you need to get an insurance policy in case you lose her. You need to bring in some other business so that you're not so reliant on just one client," he looked me in the eye. "Because you've got a problem here."

"I know I've got a problem," I admitted. "I can't stand her."

"No," he shook his head. "You've got a bigger problem because *you* can't stand her."

"I know," I agreed reluctantly.

"Have you ever heard the phrase 'if you don't like someone then they don't like you'?" he asked.

"No."

"If you can't stand her, how do you think she feels about you?"

"She probably can't stand me either," I shrugged.

BUTCHER'S WISDOM

If you don't like someone then they don't like you.

"Can you afford for your biggest client not to like you right now?"

"Of course not."

"What would happen if you lost this client?"

I thought for a moment. "Well, we wouldn't be as successful.

I might have to lay off someone I hired. She's a big chunk of change for us."

"Sounds to me like you need to find the like," he told me. "Obviously, if she's your biggest client, there was some point in your relationship where you two liked each other. You need to remember what you did like about her and try to get back to it. It may seem like she's the one not tolerant of you, but listening to you talk about her doesn't sound like you are very tolerant of her either."

The truth of Dad's statement was hard to swallow.

But at least I began chewing on it during the 20 minute drive from my parents' farm back to work. I kept trying to figure out how I was going to "find the like" in Lisa Gray.

As I walked into the office, the most profound impact of the conversation with Dad hit me.

It was Monday, perhaps the worst day of the week for me to have left the office for an hour, because the front room was filled with applicants responding to our Sunday newspaper want-ads. As I approached the front desk I heard Carrie, one of our staffers, wrapping up what sounded like a heated telephone conversation.

"Well, I am really sorry but I can't help that!" she said loudly, within earshot of everyone in the front office. "Okay, then, I'll see what I can do." She slammed the phone down.

"Who was that?" I asked her, painfully aware that all of the applicants could hear everything.

"Lisa Gray." She rolled her eyes.

"Lisa-Gray-our-biggest-client?" I asked her. "*That* Lisa Gray?"

"Yes," she said loudly. "She is such a—"

Before the big "b" word could come out of her mouth I attempted to finish Carrie's sentence for her.

"Challenge!" I interjected.

I shook my head incredulously. "I can't believe this. I am so sorry!"

Carrie and the other staff members looked at me as if I had two heads.

"What are you sorry for?" Carrie said, "She's the bitch!"

"No. I am sorry," I said. "We really do need to have a mini-meeting, right here, right now. I really have messed up this time!"

I called over to Julie, our second staffer, apologized to all of the applicants for the delay and asked the temporary receptionist to hold down the fort for a minute while we held an impromptu meeting.

As soon as we were behind closed doors, I apologized again. "Okay, team! Here is what I am sorry for. I am really sorry that I have led the way in making it okay to so dislike Lisa Gray. I'm the manager here and I own this problem. I'm completely responsible for the fact that you two think it's okay to call our biggest client a bitch, much less even think it," I nodded. "I own this because I've allowed my personal dislike of Lisa to show up right in front of the both of you. I have to tell you, I just had a conversation that was a real eye-opener for me. Have either of you ever heard the phrase *if you don't like someone then they don't like you*?"

They both shook their heads.

"I know none of us likes Lisa Gray right now and, as a result, there's a good chance—especially after that last conversation—that she doesn't like us either. Do you realize what would happen if we lost her as a client? We love our bonuses, awards and recognition, but if we lose Lisa Gray, we're going to fall pretty far, pretty fast!" I told them.

"So, what are we supposed to do?" Julie asked. "She is pretty impossible to deal with, you know."

Boy did I know it, I thought to myself, but I also thought

of my Dad's advice to "find the like," and out of thin air the words started coming.

"Here is what we are going to do. We are going to figure out a way to 'Find the Like' in Lisa Gray. We are going to start a 'Find the Like in Lisa campaign'."

I grabbed the candy dish off my desk, dumped out the candy and said, "From now on, any time anyone says or even thinks something negative about Lisa, they put a quarter in the dish. And anytime you find a way to think or say something positive about her—and tell all of us about it—you can take a quarter out. Whoever ends up with the most quarters at the end of the week wins."

They had incredulous looks on their faces.

"Believe me," I said, "I've belittled her plenty, out loud and in my own mind, and I'm the one who has allowed it to go on this long, so I'm going to start the kitty."

I took out all the quarters I had in my wallet and dumped them in the candy dish.

From that point on, we worked very hard to find the like every time we talked to her. We asked her questions that helped us figure her out a little better, questions that focused on the positives and provided answers that reminded us of the things we liked about her when we were first getting to know her. We asked her questions that let her know that we really were interested in how she was and what we could do to serve her better. We also tried to get to know her as a person so that we could find even more common ground. In one of our conversations, for example, we found out that she collected miniature dollhouses.

I'll never forget the moment that I knew we'd arrived, that we were back in a place with Lisa where we all genuinely "liked" each other. It was Christmas. Business was booming, and I can honestly say we enjoyed working with her again. Six months earlier, we would have been terrified to have been stuck in an elevator with her. Now, we actually enjoyed her company.

That year for Christmas we did not give Lisa Gray the desktop clock that was issued to us as the standard customer "corporate" gift. Instead, we gave her a tiny baby crib for her dollhouse, and she actually cried when she opened it.

We knew it was something she wanted because we had asked her what she enjoyed doing outside the office, and she told us about her passion for miniatures and that she had spent an entire weekend looking all over for a baby crib to put in the nursery of her miniature dollhouse, but could not find one.

Well, we found one. When we gave it to her, she knew not only that we listened, but also that we listened well, and she was grateful.

She remained one of our biggest customers until her company moved their headquarters to another state and she moved with them. When she left us, we truly missed her because we had come to really like her.

That is why Dad's advice hit home with me. The wisdom he shared that day when he said, "If you don't like someone then they don't like you," meant I had work to do. "Find the Like" meant I had to take action. I was responsible for looking for the good stuff to offset the bad.

A while back, when I began to look for formal coach training, I took a course at the College of Executive Coaching. One entire day of the seven-day program was spent on a concept called Appreciative Inquiry.

I now know that books have been written on this subject, but I honestly had never heard of that expression till then. In a nutshell, here is what I took away from the session: Appreciative Inquiry is all about looking for the positives and not allowing yourself to get caught up in the negatives. One example the instructor gave resonated with me.

You come home from this week-long class, she said, and

someone asks you, "How was it?" and your response is, "Great, except for Tuesday." Now, the typical next question is "What happened on Tuesday that was so bad?" And then the conversation goes the direction of all things bad. The good things that happened on the other six days get lost in a sea of badness. We tend to focus only on Bad Tuesday, and the conversation never gets back to the good stuff. It is human nature to ask about the juicy bad stuff first. It is the way most of us are programmed.

In order to get out of that way of thinking many of us have to do some self-reprogramming.

Suppose the same person asking the question "How was it?" was programmed to look for the good news first, to practice the art of Appreciative Inquiry. As soon as they heard the response, "Great, except for Tuesday," they would reply, "Well, we'll get to Tuesday in a bit, but first I want you to tell me what was great about the other six days."

I know my Father had only an eighth-grade education but I remember sitting in the room with all the Doctors and PhD's at the Executive Coaching College, years after I was introduced to the concept of "Find the Like," thinking that through his actions Dad could have taught them all a few things about Appreciative Inquiry.

He would say it so simply, "Steer the conversation toward 'finding the like.'"

BUTCHER'S WISDOM

You've gotta find the like.

Chapter Six:

Admit your Mistakes

Often, we are tested. Frequently, we experience unwelcome situations that we ourselves have created, like the mess I got myself in to with Lisa Gray.

After we initiated the "Find the Like in Lisa" campaign, I called Dad to invite him to lunch specifically to tell him the story of how I handled my problem with her. Frankly, I was pretty proud of myself and I wanted to brag a bit.

I met him at the Coyote Grill, one of my favorite celebration lunch spots, and relayed the story in record time. I told him all about the drive back to the office, walking in on Carrie slamming down the phone, my apology to the team and our plan of attack to get back on track with Lisa that was working so well.

"What do you think of that, Dad?" I asked as I finished my story.

"As usual, I am proud of you," he replied "just as I am proud of all my children when they do well."

Dad rarely gave an individual compliment to me that did not include a reminder that he was proud of all his children. Even if the accomplishment was completely mine, somehow, some way he would find a way to take whatever good he heard and spread it around. You would think I might feel slighted but I didn't. I just felt I was in good company.

He went on to say, "And what I am most proud of is the way you raised your hand, put it down and got back to playing the game."

"What do you mean by that?" I asked.

"When you acknowledged to your team that you were the one to blame for the problem with your client, you took the first step in moving forward by admitting your mistake and taking ownership," he continued. "I call that raising your hand, putting it down and getting back to playing the game."

"I still don't get it, Dad," I said. "Where did you come up with that phrase?"

"From basketball" he replied. "When I watched your brother Jerry play on the high school varsity basketball team," he went on to explain, "if a player fouled another player, the referee would blow his whistle, call 'Foul!' and point to the player who committed the foul. The guilty player would raise his hand to acknowledge his error, put his hand back down, and get back into the game."

"So, what did that accomplish?" I asked.

"It accomplished a number of things. It cleared the air in everyone's mind, players and spectators."

"How did it do that?"

"When the guilty player raised his hand, he acknowledged to everyone—to his teammates, the opposing team, and the audience—that he did it. He committed a foul."

"Okay, Dad, so that's the first thing. What else?"

"That player, then, could move on. He could get back into the game and play his best. It's like when he raised his hand, he confessed his sin to everyone, everyone forgave him, and they could all get back to what they came there for, to see a good basketball game."

"What has that got to do with us in the office? We are not playing basketball."

"The same idea holds everywhere. When you make a mistake in the office, you need to raise your hand and let everyone know it was you who made the mistake. You need to admit it. Then, everyone can move on and get back to doing their jobs. That is exactly what you did with your client situation and that is exactly what you have to remember to keep doing in order to set the right kind of example in your office."

"That's true, Dad, but people don't like to admit to making a mistake; I for one don't like to admit making a mistake."

"That's right," he said, "and that is part of the beauty of forcing yourself to admit mistakes when you make them. It also forces you to think about what you need to do in order NOT to make that same mistake again, because down deep you don't like raising your hand. Nobody does."

I agreed.

He went on, "If you don't admit it—if you don't raise your hand—you might be tempted to hide your mistake, get angry and try to bluff your way out of it, or try to figure out who you could put the blame on. If you preoccupy your mind with anything like that, you can't really get back into the game with a clear head and a focused spirit. You'll only be half there. The other half of you will be trying to figure out how to express your anger, embarrassment or frustration."

BUTCHER'S WISDOM

Raise your hand, put it down, and get back to playing the game.

"Dad, did you ever use this technique yourself?"

"Sure. Many times at work one or other of us would make a mistake—we'd make a wrong cut on a beautiful side of beef, or we'd slice up two pounds of the most expensive ham when all the customer wanted was ordinary baloney. I told my workers, when they made mistakes, to mention it to the rest of the team, so we would all know why there was two pounds of expensive ham all sliced up sitting in the display case, or why this side of beef was cut wrong. People make mistakes. People will always make mistakes. What keeps the game from being played—and the shop from running well—is when people try to hide their mistakes and not accept responsibility for them."

"Are you saying that people are more willing to forgive and forget your mistakes, if you openly admit them?"

"I certainly am. It's only a very small-minded person who will hold onto resentments when someone admits a mistake. Since your brothers knew the hand-raising technique from basketball, they used the approach at the butcher shop all the time. Whenever one of the boys made a mistake, raising their hand to admit it made for great fellowship at the market, especially with my other employees. Expecting my sons to admit their mistakes openly and not to hide them went a long way to show everybody on our team that I did not play favorites. Everyone got into the spirit of forgiveness, because they all wanted to play the game more than they wanted to blame their teammates or fill their hearts with anger and frustration."

"Did you ever have workers in the shop who tried to hide their mistakes?"

"Sure. Those were the times I had to play the role of referee. I had to coach the guy who messed up how to raise his hand, admit his error, then put his hand back down and get to work."

"What would you say to him?"

"I would tell him that we were a team here, that we were more focused on getting work done and pleasing the customers than we were about punishing employees for making mistakes. I would tell him that the other workers would always raise their hands when they made a mistake, just like at high school basketball games, and then we would all get right back to work."

"Dad, I don't see the hand-raising at basketball games these days."

"You're right. I don't know when they did away with that rule, if it ever was an official rule, but it seems that good sportsmanship lost out when they stopped doing it."

"I agree," I said. "Nowadays, I see basketball players angrily arguing with the referee when a foul is called on them. They vehemently deny that they committed the foul, or they claim it was somebody else's fault—never theirs."

"And if you watch these players," my Dad said, "you can see them carrying their anger as they run down the court, their minds more on their anger than on the ball."

Dad was right again, I thought. I am sure there are times when the accused player did not commit the foul, when the ref was wrong, but from what I had seen there had never been one case that I knew of when a basketball player argued with the ref and his call was reversed.

I did not know much about the game of basketball, but I knew that when you were in a situation that you did not have any control over at the office and a "foul" was called on you, carrying your anger around about the mistake never did any good.

I knew I needed to find a way to take this latest "Butcher's Wisdom" and apply it in my office, but I wasn't sure Dad's sports phrase would hit home with my female co-workers who were even less sports-minded than I was. I would need to figure out a way to communicate Dad's wisdom with slightly different words. And then I met Dee Dee.

Dee Dee was the Branch Manager of the Milwaukee office and a real "spark plug." When I met her the first time at a regional meeting, her energy and especially her smile lit up the room. She was my peer and I could tell she was also a kindred spirit, so I hoped that our paths would cross often because I knew she was someone I could learn from.

I got my wish shortly after our first encounter. Ray, our regional Vice President, asked Dee Dee and me to make a joint presentation at our next national meeting. Ray had been impressed with both of us when he visited our offices. He was especially delighted by the way we both "built loyalty" with our clients and temporaries, and asked us in our presentation to share our customer service secrets with our colleagues in the business.

We were both honored and nervous.

Ray coached us on insights we might want to include in our presentation, things that he had observed in both of us as he watched us in action during his visits to our offices.

"Dee Dee," he said, "I think it is very important that you talk about the mirror. I think it is one of the keys to your success."

"The mirror?" I questioned out loud.

"The mirror," Ray replied, smiling at Dee Dee.

"Okay," Dee Dee began. "Here is how I use the mirror. I keep a mirror on my desk to the right of my phone, for two reasons. One, it helps me remember to smile whenever I answer the phone or carry on a conversation. This makes for a more pleasant exchange for both of us on the line." She turned to me and said, "I'm sure you can tell when the person at the other end of the line is smiling versus when they are frowning? I know I can, so I smile every chance I get."

"You should," I replied. "You have one of the most beautiful smiles I have ever seen."

"Thanks!" She beamed, blushed and added, "I practice a lot."

"And the second reason for the mirror?" Ray prodded.

"To remind me to admit my mistakes and move on," Dee Dee replied. "In fact, on Ray's suggestion, we all now have mirrors on our desks in our office for that very reason. When something goes wrong, for example, when a temp doesn't show up for an assignment or a client gets angry about a mismatch, we all realize that the best way to deal with the problem is to 'look in the mirror.' It's hard at times NOT to blame the unreliable temp or the crazy client, but it never does any good when you do. Blaming someone else is never a productive use of our energy. What is productive when things go wrong is to begin with the premise that the first step in moving ahead and learning from it is to 'look in the mirror' and ask yourself, 'What could I have said and what could I have done that could have changed the outcome?' Once you do that, you focus all your energy on what you can control, which is nothing but you and your actions."

"I love it," I replied. "It is exactly the phrase I was looking for to help me own up to 'my bads' and to use with my team. I am definitely sharing with my own team the idea of 'look in the mirror,'" I said.

And I did. I bought mirrors for every staff member.

The first time I used the mirror on my desk to remind me to smile, when I would have preferred to tell someone off, it hit me. Dee Dee's mirror technique for staying focused in the office was much the same as my Dad's butcher wisdom for staying focused in the shop—and on the basketball court. "Raise your hand, put it down, and get back to playing the game."

CHAPTER SEVEN:

Enjoy the Ride

NEARLY FIVE YEARS INTO MY CAREER, things were going very, very well for me—so well, in fact, that I referred to my work life as "Camelot."

Things were as right in my work world as they could possibly be. The company was growing and so was I. I had been promoted to the role of Midwest area manager, and I had been recognized time and time again for my achievements.

I was also tapped regularly to help train new managers and consult with other offices outside my area. This meant that I got to do a lot of traveling—something that I very much enjoyed.

As a result of my travels, I was starting to taste a lot of the finer things in life. At the courtesy of my company, I often flew first-class to meetings and recognition events, and I would stay at some of the nicest hotels and resorts. They were a far cry from the Travelodge's of my youth—certainly fancier than anything I thought I would ever be exposed to, even in my wildest adolescent dreams.

Just when I thought life couldn't get much better, I was asked to represent my company in their international exchange program. This meant I was going to spend six weeks working as the exchange manager in one of our sister offices in Great Britain.

Needless to say, I was ecstatic to have been given the opportunity, and I invited my parents to accompany me during my first week abroad on holiday in London.

Although I was excited, I was a little apprehensive about spending so many weeks completely alone in a foreign country, and it was very comforting to me to have my parents accompany me during the beginning of my stay.

We traveled in November of 1985, just as the Christmas shopping season was beginning. On the plane ride over, my mom had compiled a gift list a mile long.

In London, she was thrilled to find Cabbage Patch dolls for her grandchildren, as they were impossible to get in the States that year. Fortunately, they were in abundance in the London stores. Because she had nine granddaughters at that time, she soon had a wealth of Cabbage Patch dolls in her hotel room.

We did a lot of sightseeing that week, but I think Mom was most in her element buying gifts for others. As a result, we spent a good deal of time shopping together.

Dad was another story. People-watching was his thing. Observing him operate in a completely new environment was fascinating to me. He was busy all the time, striking up conversations, making new acquaintances, asking people questions about their businesses and their lives.

He was ready to meet and chat with anyone, anywhere and everywhere. Whenever we got into a cab, right off he would ask the driver where he was from, how long had he been living there, did his family like it there, what did they like most. He would comment to the hotel check-in staff how lucky they were to work in such a beautiful hotel, or tell a waitress how lovely her smile was. He was no different from the way he was at home. I wondered whether people in a big city would react positively to some happy guy pointing out all the positives around him, but they did.

He was both inquisitive and charming at the same time, and people spontaneously opened up to him revealing anything and everything he wanted to know.

His ability to do this—to anyone and everyone—really amazed me.

As I watched the way he so easily endeared himself to people, I felt very proud of him, except when he tried to get the guards at Buckingham Palace to talk to him. Not his best decision. As everyone knows, they are ordered as part of their job NOT to reply to tourists who talk to them. He just couldn't understand that a human being wasn't allowed to talk—or wouldn't respond to him—and continued to attempt to engage the guards in conversation. He asked them questions about their health and about how their backs must be hurting after standing at attention so long. He questioned how often they got breaks, etc., etc. They never budged, never spoke or smiled. It really bothered him that he could not get any reaction at all.

But I have to admit that going into the trip I did not know whether I would be proud of his behavior or embarrassed by it. I half expected that everyone would react to him the way the guards at the palace did. To be honest, I was a bit afraid that he would not act or dress appropriately and that his over-friendly Kansas style would be perceived as intrusive—too *American*—in this different culture.

As it turned out, nothing could have been further from the truth. The same principles he followed at home for connecting with people worked just as well in London. The first hunk of meat he sold was himself, and he poured on the comeback sauce everywhere we went. And, aside from the guards at Buckingham Palace, people just loved him for it.

In fact, I found myself growing a little jealous because he seemed to be spreading so much of his attention over all these other new people and not spending time with me. This week was supposed to be *my* time with *my* parents, two-on-one for the first time in my life. I was not at all sure I was happy about sharing my father with strangers.

Two days before my parents were scheduled to head back to the States and I was scheduled to formally start work in my new office, we all went on a shopping trip to Harrods, the famous department store in London that has everything you could ever want to buy all under one roof, including a fabulous meat department.

My mother and I spent most of our time gift shopping for the nieces, nephews and grandkids. When it was time to leave Harrods, I told my mother to wait in a department where she would be kept occupied, and went looking for Dad. Of course, I found him in their meat department chatting over the counter with the head butcher.

From what I remember it was called something like a "Grand Hall" in Harrods that housed all the meat, produce, baked goods and groceries. Even though it was downstairs, it still had high ceilings with beautiful light fixtures and lots of marble and tile floors. I definitely remember it feeling very grand! Bichelmeyer Meats in Kansas, on the other hand, had more of the local butcher shop feel with packages rolled up in white wax paper and tied with string, compared to the beautiful striped Harrods bags people carried their food home in.

As I walked up to my father, he introduced me to the head butcher from Harrods, and the gentleman greeted me as if I were the daughter of royalty. I had no idea what my father had told him about his meat business. We chatted a bit more, and my father proudly told him that I would be working in his country, representing the entire United States. The way he described me, you'd think I was the U.S. Ambassador to Great Britain. I guess the way my father saw it, I *was* a U.S. Ambassador to Great Britain, just as he was during his stay with me.

As we were leaving, we said our good-byes to all the meat department staff. Then, much to my dismay, I realized that Dad had made arrangements to meet the head butcher the following morning at 5:30 at Covent Garden and make the rounds with him at the daily local growers' meat selection and pick-up.

"What are you doing, Dad?" I asked as we walked away. "Tomorrow will be our last full day together," I said, unable to hide my disappointment. "We were supposed to take a drive to Stratford together."

"We'll still be able to do that," he assured me. "But I really want to ride along with this man in the morning. I think there is a lot I could learn from the experience."

"But Dad, this trip was supposed to be about spending time with me!" I said. I knew that I was playing the role of the hurt little girl at that moment, but I didn't care. "I really want to spend time with you!"

"Then come along with me in the morning. Then we can all take the ride to the country together in the afternoon." He smiled at me and winked. "You never know, you might learn something too," he said. "I have always believed that you can learn something from every person you meet."

BUTCHER'S WISDOM

Learn something from every person you meet.

I sighed. How could I not agree? The very thought of going to an early morning wholesale meat market—in London—made him glow with happiness.

On the other hand, I began to calculate how early I would have to set my alarm to have enough time to get dressed and get to Covent Garden by 5:30. Dad never liked to be late for any event.

So I got up in what seemed like the middle of the night, dressed warmly in a pair of jeans and my brand new fuzzy thigh-length turtleneck sweater. I pulled on brown leather ankle boots I had purchased at Harrods the day before and met him in the lobby. Dad had on his new camel hair sports coat purchased in the hotel gift shop, his usual crisp white dress shirt and bolero tie. It remained his uniform—his dress outfit—for years after we got home. On his head he wore a brand new fedora, and he carried Mom's new Burberry umbrella, because, as he had noticed, "That's what people did in London."

Outside the hotel, we hopped in a cab—he loved the old-fashioned black taxi cabs there because they were so easy to get in and out of—and told the driver to take us to Covent Garden to meet the head butcher. He was as excited as a kid in a candy store with ten dollars in his pocket. He couldn't wait to get there.

We found the butcher from Harrods intensely negotiating with a vendor over a cut of beef. Since he was so busy buying what he needed for the day, we kept out of his way and mostly watched the people swarming around, shouting, waving arms, giving commands and pointing here and there.

It turned out that I did learn something on that adventure with my father, not so much while we were in the midst of the loud, chaotic and smelly experience at Covent Garden, but from the time we shared afterward, over our breakfast.

We had spent over two pre-dawn hours among all the farmers and craftsmen setting up for their day of trade. In the midst of all the hectic and, for many, back-breaking work, we could feel a happy atmosphere of greetings, camaraderie, and laughter, people enjoying not only what they were doing, but interested in what others were doing as well. The merchants and suppliers expressed a deep kinship with each other. To my surprise, the morning turned out to be a really enjoyable experience.

"That was fun," Dad said as we devoured a traditional English breakfast of tomatoes, eggs, bacon and beans. Both of us were in hog heaven.

The autumn sun was rising over London, as we looked out the window of the restaurant a few blocks from the wholesalers market.

"Could you believe all those people unloading their trucks and getting ready for market, getting ready to show the world their wares?" he asked.

His pleasure being in those surroundings was obvious.

"Yes, Dad," I admitted. "It was fun. But I'm curious what made it that way for you?"

I asked him, really wanting to know exactly what he thought was so great about what we just did. I honestly wasn't sure I really understood why it was so much fun and why he wanted me there, too!

"Well," he said, eagerly cutting up his eggs, "I think it was fun because we were around a lot of people who were finding their happiness in the pursuit," he said. "And I think we both got caught up in it, don't you?" he asked.

I admitted that I had felt the excitement and energy of the place.

"Did you notice we did not come across anyone who was cranky or ugly to us or to each other? They were all too busy working and laughing and enjoying their pursuit."

"I'm not sure I get what you mean by 'finding their happiness in the pursuit,'" I said. I watched him sprinkle salt on his tomato and relish a bite of it.

"I can't believe you haven't heard me say that before," he commented.

"I probably did, Dad, but I was probably too young at the time to get it."

At that moment, however, I was all ears.

"I believe that more than anything else," he said, looking me straight in the eye, "it's not the pursuit of happiness but the *happiness of pursuit* that inspires people."

"The happiness of pursuit?" I asked.

"Yes. I think the happiest people are the ones who are inspired and enjoying the ride they are on *while they are on it*," he said.

BUTCHER'S WISDOM

It's not the pursuit of happiness but the happiness of pursuit that inspires.

When he said the word "ride," I knew he meant the ride called life. You couldn't enjoy life on this earth before you were born, and you sure couldn't enjoy it after it was over.

"And I think," he went on, "that we create our good times by realizing that and living a life that supports it—living a life well lived."

"What do you mean by 'living a life well lived?'" I asked him. "How does somebody do that?"

"I never really thought about the how," he said. "But now that you ask, I think it's pretty simple."

"I need you to spell it out for me, please," I said as I sipped on my wonderfully strong and aromatic English breakfast tea.

"Well, first, I think you have to keep busy because 'idle time is the devil's workshop.' And if you keep busy, you can keep the devil away. Your mind won't wander into the 'Woe is me!' mentality. Besides, it's hard not to feel good about yourself when you're doing something productive."

BUTCHER'S WISDOM

Stay Busy. Idle time is the devil's workshop.

"That's pretty clear," I admitted, "so far."

"Next, I'd say you have to take the time to appreciate what the good Lord and everyone around you has given you, and not act like it's your due. I think you have to take every chance you get to say 'thank you'."

BUTCHER'S WISDOM

Don't act like it's your due—take every chance to say thank you.

"So, a life well lived means being productive and grateful," I said. "Is that it?"

"No, that's not everything. After that, I would say that you need to be careful not to get all wrapped up in yourself—especially when things are going well and you might be thinking you are pretty hot stuff— because you know, 'when you're all wrapped up in yourself, you make a damn small package.'"

BUTCHER'S WISDOM

When you're all wrapped up in yourself
you make a damn small package.

At this point, he stopped for a moment to think. I could tell his mind was working when his eyes drifted upward as if he was looking at some distant object.

"Last but not least and maybe most important," he went on to say. "You always have to remember that nobody makes you happy but yourself."

BUTCHER'S WISDOM

Nobody makes you happy
but yourself.

"Come on, Dad," I said, "you have been making people

happy all your life. How can you say that nobody makes you happy but yourself?"

"All I can do for someone else is to help bring a smile to their face. The happiness I generate is just momentary. When I say 'happiness' I'm thinking about a kind of permanent attitude."

"So, you don't think other people can truly make you happy?"

"Well, it sure helps if people are nice to you and delight you," he said, "but happiness comes first from inside a person, not from the outside."

"I guess that's right," I said.

"Sure, it's right," he said emphatically. "Have you ever noticed that the people who are always looking for someone else to complete them or to be the answer to their prayers for happiness never seem to be able to find happiness?" he said. "Maybe for a short time they get a glimmer of it, but then, somehow, some way, the person they were counting on lets them down and they are unhappy again. Why do you think that is?" he asked.

He didn't wait for my response.

He said, "It's because they are always looking outside of themselves for happiness and they don't get the fact that nobody can make you happy but yourself."

At that moment I remember feeling so grateful that this incredible man was my father, and that, somehow I had managed to get him alone, one-on-one, for a few precious hours that I would never forget.

"Thanks, Dad," I said and smiled at him.

"For what?" he asked.

"I don't know where to start," I said. "For this morning, for breakfast, for our time together. For everything."

"You're welcome," he said as he reached across the table and covered my hand with his.

"I love you, Papa," I said.

"I love you too," he responded. "Now, let's get back to your mother before she starts to worry about us."

What good times those were. What cherished memories I have. What a stack of Butcher's Wisdom from a single breakfast!

CHAPTER EIGHT:

Look for Happiness Within

AFTER OUR INCREDIBLE WEEK TOGETHER IN ENGLAND, Mom and Dad had flown back to the States and I was left to carry on the rest of my adventure alone.

It was now up to me to follow my father's advice and stay focused on all the principles he taught me so that I would continue to find the happiness in the pursuit.

The day before I was to start work in my exchange office, I was invited to have dinner with two of the top company executives.

I remember feeling very intimidated and needing to psyche myself up for the meeting. As I was getting ready, I kept telling myself over and over, "I can do this! I can do this!"

And I did!

I successfully navigated the London public transportation system from my hotel to the restaurant. I took the subway, the "tube" as they call it in London. I remember getting a kick out of the phrase "Mind the gap" when the doors of the subway train would close. Back in the States, I would often repeat to others "Mind the gap" in my best English accent whenever I could.

I easily made it in time for dinner with the CEO and the CFO of the company.

As I was walking into the restaurant, I recalled one of my Dad's sayings from breakfast the day before.

BUTCHER'S WISDOM

The happiest people are the ones who are inspired and enjoying the ride they are on while they are on it.

"I'm on a wonderful ride," I said to myself.

I was completely in awe of the restaurant—talk about surroundings! This place was nothing short of opulent. I felt like Princess Diana herself. We dined on peppercorn steak in a mahogany-paneled room and I was on cloud nine the whole time. The place was very intimate and quiet. Linen tablecloths, linen napkins, genuine silver silverware.

The gentlemen I sat next to ordered everything, cocktails before dinner—some sort of whiskey on ice, no mixer—wine with dinner specifically selected to complement their meals, and then some sort of after dinner drink with cream, like a Baileys. I never drank "highballs," as my Dad called them, so when they asked me what I wanted, I asked for wine.

I am still not very well-educated in wines, and as I was not a big drinker at that time, even at company functions back home, I would always ask for a glass of champagne because I liked the long and lean glass it came in. But at that time in that restaurant, I knew nothing about wine!

They asked what I wanted to drink and I said, "A glass of wine, please." And with that I thought I had completed my order.

The next obvious question came, "Red or white?" I had heard somewhere you had red with steak, so I said red and when the next question came regarding the type, I looked at Alfred the CEO and said, "What do you suggest?" At that point I had him.

All of us at our table ordered peppercorn steak because the place was famous for it.

The two officers (CEO and CFO) were both in their 40's and very well dressed, pinstripe suits and tie. One was a very attractive man, the other not all that attractive but both were nicely put together. Both were very sophisticated. I loved their accents and I could have listened to them all night.

I had on my very best brand new black suit purchased at Barkers in Kensington, which at the time I thought was pretty high line. Now I know it is only a step above Target here. But what did I care? I had bought a business suit in London. I thought I looked like a million bucks even though I am sure the total cost of the entire ensemble was less than $100.

At the end of the evening, I mentally patted myself on the back for a job well done. Here I was, this skinny hick from Kansas, and I had successfully convinced the company "big dogs" that I was intelligent, witty and charming!

After dinner was over, we said our goodbyes. As they opened the door for me, they both took turns at taking shaking my hand and kissing my cheek. They seemed genuinely grateful for our time together.

I said my thanks and good-byes, assuring the gentlemen that I could manage on my own, and set out for the "tube" station, feeling very confident.

"Whew! What a relief!" I thought to myself. "That went really well!"

I went on my merry way, smiling from ear-to-ear at anyone who looked at me as I walked and as I sat on the subway train because I was so pleased with myself. I just knew that I had been perceived as both engaging and entertaining. It had been the perfect evening all around. On the way back to my hotel, it felt like I was floating on a sea of contentment.

As I was getting ready for bed, I walked in to the bathroom thinking that these were indeed good and happy times.

I looked in the mirror and smiled at myself.

That is when I saw it.

There it was, wedged right smack-dab in the center of my two front teeth, a huge chunk of pepper staring back at me! It almost looked as if I had blacked out my two front teeth. I mean, it was *huge!*

I realized there is no way that it could have gone unnoticed by my executive companions.

At first, I just wanted to die right then and there, but then I just shook my head and laughed out loud, recalling my father's advice from the day before.

"You're right, Dad," I thought to myself, as I brushed my teeth. "'Nobody can make you happy but yourself.'"

Truth be told, in spite of that hunk of pepper, I was a very happy girl. I was seriously enjoying the ride I was on, and grateful to be on it.

CHAPTER NINE:

Celebrate Life

MY FATHER KNEW ROUGH TIMES. He was born in a cabin with a dirt floor in Eudora, Kansas that he shared with his grandparents from Germany, his mother and father and their growing family. At an early age, he learned to trap and hunt for food. When game was scarce, he might pick potatoes for a neighbor to help feed his nine brothers and sisters.

At age 14, at the beginning of the Great Depression, he graduated from grade school and left home to find work. Like his father and grandfather before him, he planned to make his living in the meat business. He never went to high school.

By 1946, he was married with three children and had realized his dream of opening his own butcher shop, but five years later, about the same time his sixth child was born, a flood wiped out Bichelmeyer Meats, and he had to start all over again. Despite these rough times, he always seemed to be happy.

No matter what he did or did not have financially, Dad was always reminding us by his actions that the happiest people are the ones who are inspired and enjoying the ride they are on while they are on it."

By the time I came along in 1958 our family was experiencing the best of times financially. The meat market was prospering as were the real estate investments my father had made. Mom and Dad had built their dream home on a farm in Shawnee, Kansas the year before I was born. We had our own livestock on the property—cattle, horses, pigs and chickens as well as a vegetable garden that could feed our family, with tomatoes and cucumbers to spare.

But to hear my older siblings tell their stories, even when times were tough, they never felt that they were doing without because Mom and Dad always found a way to celebrate life every chance they got.

Other than Christmas, which was a huge event for all of us, my favorite traditions were our birthday celebrations and "Sunday Fun Day." My sister Judy, my oldest living sibling, recalls Sunday Fun Days as some of her happiest early childhood memories.

In a nut-shell, a Sunday Fun Day was a day of celebration. EVERY Sunday Dad took off work and we all went to church together in the morning. After Mass, we headed to the store of our choice to select our Sunday Fun Day prize. Some weeks it was the toy store or the local "Five and Dime," and sometimes it was just the local grocery where we bought a big bag of our favorite candy, but every Sunday we got to pick a prize "just because," as Dad would say.

I remember having Sunday Fun Day withdrawals when I moved away from home to college. I think my roommate Karen thought I was crazy the first time I suggested we go out on a Sunday and buy ourselves a small prize "just because." However, it didn't take long for her to catch on, and soon we had half the girls on our floor tagging along on our Sunday celebrations.

BUTCHER'S WISDOM

Celebrate every chance you get.

Because I had grown up with a "celebrate every chance you get" mentality, I found it especially difficult when I started working to understand how so many people around me chose not to draw attention to milestone events and celebrate them.

I will never forget my first birthday on the job. No one did anything to celebrate it! I knew that about a week before the big day I had mentioned to Sam and Lily that my birthday was coming up, but after that I never mentioned it again. On my actual birthday, we were so busy staffing a huge inventory project for a client that my birthday was completely forgotten. And I never said a word about it to anyone that day.

I left work and drove to my parents' house for my family birthday celebration. Since every family member's birthday was celebrated each year as a big event at our house, I knew I was in for a good time.

However, remembering my day at work, I was still feeling hurt and resentful. "How dare they forget my birthday!" I thought to myself, "After all I do for the two of them!" Quite the martyr, I thought about quitting my job the next day. I even concocted a resignation speech on the way home. "After all I have done for the two of you, I can't believe you forgot my birthday" was how I planned to begin.

I walked in to Mom's kitchen and the smell of stuffed

peppers met me at the door. I should have felt better immediately knowing that Mom had lovingly prepared my favorite birthday meal of stuffed peppers, mashed potatoes, corn and 'Aunt Bertille's' famous chocolate cake for dessert, but I didn't. One phase of each person's birthday celebration was having Mom prepare that person's favorite meal.

Dad was sitting at the butcher block reading the evening newspaper by himself because Mom had to run to the store to get some fresh bread.

"How has your birthday gone so far?" Dad asked.

I burst in to tears.

"What birthday?" I sobbed. "It might as well have been any other day of the year because nobody in the office said or did a thing for me!"

He listened quietly as I went on with my sob story.

"Can you believe it, Dad?" I asked through my tears. "I feel like going in there tomorrow morning and quitting. This just proves that they don't appreciate me at all."

"You are not going to get any sympathy from me on this one, young lady," he said. "I say that if somebody close to you forgets your birthday, it's your own damn fault."

His response took me completely by surprise. Let me preface this by saying that Dad rarely used any foul language around me so you can imagine how shocked I felt. Here I was expecting sympathy from him, and his reply was quite the opposite.

He went on to ask, "Why in the world didn't you walk in your office first thing this morning and announce to all within earshot that it was your big day and you fully expected it to be special and you were wondering what the heck they were all going to do to make it that way?"

Not the response I expected, but a life lesson I never forgot!

Since that day, March 24th 1981, I can tell you that

without exception I have NEVER had a birthday that I did not celebrate in a big way with the help of everyone around me. I made sure that all those likely to be around me that day did not have even the remote possibility of forgetting my birthday. The tradition also extended to elaborate birthday celebrations for all those closest to me at work or at home. If you were on a team I worked with, you could be assured that you were never slighted on your big day. The day I either hired or inherited a team member, their birthday went on the calendar with reminders noted not only on THE day but three days before so preparations would not wait till the last minute. The same rule was put in place for company anniversaries.

While for me the "blinders" is the hardest principle to follow consistently that Dad taught me, "celebrate every chance you get" is the easiest. At work and at home, I love following this bit of wisdom. In my little world I am kind of famous for it.

I remember when I was promoted to the role of Kansas City Area Manager and I got the bright idea that we should host a celebratory event for our clients and temporary employees to show our appreciation of them.

Never one to hold a party without a theme, I decided to set the date for the event the week of the Academy Awards. We invited all our clients and temps telling them they had been "nominated" for an award and we very much hoped to see them the night of our gala event.

The turnout was fabulous and as we handed out awards for categories like "outstanding performance by a new client" and "outstanding performance by a client that increased their business over prior year," I was amazed to watch how some of the most reserved businessmen and women I worked with responded to the celebration and our appreciation of them.

They were grateful to us because we were grateful for them. It was a beautiful thing. When both our "Client of the Year" and "Temporary of the Year" asked to do acceptance speeches when they were handed their awards, I knew that we were onto something. Naturally, the gala became an annual event. I'm certain this event became one of the key reasons our area experienced such incredible client and employee loyalty.

I have learned over the years that "celebrate every chance you get" comes easier to some than others. Because I am more of an extrovert, it is easy for me to want to be a part of a celebration and to use the principle as a motivator for my people. For most of my career I worked for people who felt the same way.

My first real challenge came when I was promoted to the role of Southern Region Vice President and I began to report to Jack.

Jack was a great guy, but he was more introverted in his leadership style than I was accustomed to. It was not so much a fault, just his style. But it made for some mismatched expectations at times, and I could see that others who watched him lead were beginning to find fault because he did not recognize and reward our team as often as we would have liked.

Shortly after I took over the southern region, I set the goal for our team to reach the milestone of 100,000 hours a week. That meant we had to have at least 2,500 temps employed in our region whose working hours during the previous week totaled up to 100,000 billable hours. That would be quite an accomplishment, because, up to that time, the region had been running at an average of around 60,000 hours a week. So, it was a stretch goal. When we hit it in record time, it was cause to celebrate.

The minute the flash report confirmed our goal had been met, the phone started ringing and faxes started flying. After the previous week's flash, we had known that the goal was close, so we were preparing for it.

To each of the offices all over the region we had pre-shipped their 100,000 Hour Celebration Box that was to be opened when it was officially announced we had met the goal.

"They are getting a 'party in a box,'" my assistant Trish would say. She filled the box with $100,000 dollar candy bars and other goodies as well as streamers and confetti. From all over the region, the response to the gesture was overwhelming. The teams loved it, but knowing them as well as I did, I expected they would. This region had turned into a group that loved to celebrate.

What I did not expect was their concern for me for what I was getting—or not getting—now that we had met our goal.

"What did Jack do when he heard the news?" one person asked. "How did Jack honor our accomplishment?" came the question in faxes and phone calls.

Now, Jack had been sent copies and notices on everything we had done to hype the goal. We even sent him his own celebration box, and I knew he received the fax announcement that the goal had been met. I also knew he was always all over those flash reports the minute they came out.

I *knew* he knew we had met the goal, yet I had not heard a word from him. I waited all that day and still no congratulatory fax or phone call. By the following morning with still no word from him, I started to feel angry and resentful.

It was then that I remembered my Dad's advice that if you don't get the celebration you want "it's your own damn fault." So I picked up the phone.

The first call I made was to the local florist where I ordered a dozen yellow roses and had them sent to my office. I asked the florist to sign the card:

To Mary and the Southern Region Team,
Congratulations on achieving your goal.
I am so proud of all of you!
Jack

The second call I made was to Jack. When his assistant put me through, the conversation went like this.

"Hi there!" I began. "How are you today?"

"Great!" he replied. "As you know, we had a solid week last week thanks in no small part to you and your team. Awesome job on that 100K week."

"Thanks, Jack." I replied. "We were so proud of ourselves when we got the news yesterday, there were celebrations going on all over the region. It was a fun day. Actually, that is the reason for my call. I did something this morning that I hope you are okay with."

"What is it?" he asked.

"I spent some of your money for you," I began. "You see, when I didn't hear from you yesterday, I was a little hurt that you did not recognize the milestone we achieved. By this morning, when that hurt started to turn in to anger, I decided to do something about it. So I picked up the phone and called my local florist and sent myself a dozen roses and signed the card from you."

I went on to say, "They are sending the bill to your office."

"As far as my team is concerned," I continued, "I am not telling anyone that I sent myself the flowers. I am just bragging to everyone about the fact that these beautiful yellow roses on my desk have come from you. Last but not least, I have drafted a letter that is perfect for you to send to all the region offices congratulating them on the achievement. I know it will mean a lot to them to hear from you."

I took a deep breath and closed with, "So that's what I did. Now, the question for you is, are you okay with that?"

There was only silence on the other end of the line.

I was worried until he finally responded, "I am more than okay with it. I am very grateful, but I am also sorry that you had to take it upon yourself to do that. I know I should be better about those things, but I just don't think that way."

"I know that, Jack," I said, "and since I *do* think that way maybe we can help each other out in this area."

"Exactly," he replied. "I know that on paper you report to me, but in this area I could use an internal coach. Would you be willing to help me out whenever you see something in the company that needs to be recognized and rewarded?" He went on, "I would really appreciate it if you would work with me as to what and how I should respond. Deal?"

"Deal!" I replied.

"Oh, and can we make one more deal?" he asked.

"Sure," I replied, "What is it?"

"You can feel free to send yourself something from time to time on my account when I forget things, but let's keep it at a dozen roses, okay? No Ferraris."

"Deal," I replied.

I hung up the phone smiling, once again grateful for the foundation of wisdom that I had learned through the years from my father. It was also the first time I realized that when I needed to I could make up my own butcher wisdom.

When I needed to, I could add one bit of wisdom to another to create a third.

Case in point:

Nobody makes you happy but yourself

+

Celebrate every chance you get =

BUTCHER'S WISDOM

Send yourself flowers.

Chapter Ten:

Put Bad Things in Perspective

By the year 2000, I was 20 years into my career and, for the most part, "still enjoying the ride," as Dad would say. I was working with people I loved and I felt appropriately rewarded for my efforts. I had established a track record of building solid teams, hiring great people and experienced virtually no voluntary turnover within my direct reports. I had made it in the people business and I was still finding all kinds of happiness in the pursuit.

As far as my home life, I had been blessed as well. My family continued to be my mainstay. My mother and father were always there when I needed them, as were my siblings and our ever-growing extended family members.

Twelve years before, in 1988, I married my husband, Scott, and we were blessed with two healthy and happy boys who grew as rapidly as the love and gratitude we felt for them.

Life had been pretty darn good to me.

It was at that blissful time that some things started to change.

The most devastating of all these changes was figuring out how to deal with the loss of my mother. She had always been my safe haven. Growing up, I was much closer to Mom than to Dad. She was always there. She represented warmth and safety and unconditional love. Of course, I do remember being disciplined by her. But when I think of her, most memories bring a smile to my face and warmth to my heart.

I had no idea how powerfully Mom's death would affect me. I had lost people I loved before: my brother Johnny, my Grandpa Matson, my nephews Justin and Ricky, and my brother-in-law Lou. But with those losses, as sad as they were, life seemed to carry on for me. The loss of my mother was a different story. I missed her so much after she was gone that I ached for her. Most of all, I missed the warmth of her touch, the feeling of safety she provided and the unconditional love she gave.

Dad did his best to pick up the extra parenting required by those of us who found ourselves feeling lost after she was gone. For me, I know lunches with Dad and funny faxes from him were more frequent than before, and trips together and phone calls to check in were made more often as well.

I found myself growing even closer to Dad since he was now my sole source of parental support. I no longer relied on him for just my work wisdom, although I certainly kept him busy dishing it out.

As it would happen, over the next few years my relatively trouble-free "Camelot" work world began to change dramatically as well.

It all began when Ray, who was now our CEO, and one of the people I admired most over my entire career, left the company after a disagreement with our Board of Directors. Needless to say, his departure was difficult for me to deal with, as well as many of the other departures that followed. One by one, people started to leave and the culture of the company I loved began to change.

Over the next few years, under the new leadership team the Board brought in, I would grow increasingly more uncomfortable with the type of company we were becoming.

In spring of 2003, after my mentor Gary decided to resign, I was at one of the lowest points of my career. After a particularly challenging executive team meeting, I remember calling Dad and asking him to join me for lunch.

We met at The Blue Moose in Prairie Village, Kansas, about two minutes from my office. Dad was 86 at that time and had been living on his own for three years since Mom passed away. He still wore a white cotton shirt, red suspenders, work jeans and his German cap.

We sat at the bar and, as usual, Dad ordered whatever German beer they had. He had a steak and mashed potatoes, and I chose a Reuben sandwich. We both tried Fried Pickles for the first time in our lives.

After we had ordered, I started right in.

"Dad, I'm not sure what to think of the company we are becoming," I shrugged. "I just got back from a meeting that really has me down. I'm really not comfortable with the direction we seem to be heading and I'm troubled by the new style of leadership."

He sensed my distress. He reached out in that familiar way of his and put his big hand over mine.

"Well," he said. "I would say you are pretty darn lucky that in all these years you've not had to deal with many bad times at work until now."

"That's true," I admitted,

"You dealt with the good times pretty well, accepted those didn't you?" he asked.

"Sure, I'm grateful for all those good years."

"Now, it sounds to me like you are just going to have to figure out how to deal with the bad."

"So, your advice here is to 'deal with it?'" I asked, almost defensively.

My Camelot work world was falling apart and his advice was to just "deal with it." I did feel a bit self-absorbed but, frankly, I had hoped for more from him than that. If I could not vent to my Dad, who could I vent to?

"Yes, you're going to have to deal with it, so deal with it," he replied with a smile. "And the first thing you obviously have to do here is lighten up a little bit. The key is to put it all in perspective," he said.

"Okay," I replied. "And how do you suggest I do that?"

"Well, before you get all caught up in what's wrong where you are now, I think you have to try and find the like," he said. "You can make yourself crazy if all you do is look at what is wrong all the time. You have to look for the good news to balance the bad in order to help you put things in perspective."

"Easier said than done." I still felt discouraged

"So let's start with a question," he began. "What is going on at work that is *right* right now?" he asked.

"Nothing," I replied instantly. "Really, nothing!" I insisted. "People are leaving right and left, the place is in chaos, we don't seem to have a consistent focus and direction anymore, and I don't particularly like the leadership styles of the new people they are bringing in." I shrugged. "I just don't believe they will be very effective leading the company their way over the long haul."

He looked at me with great compassion, but I wasn't about to be consoled.

"So there you have it, Dad," I said and then issued him a challenge. "What good can you find in that?"

He took a deep breath and kept looking at me. I thought that maybe, for once, I had actually stumped him. I wondered what good he could find in this mess I was in.

"Well," he said with a grin, "they're still paying you, aren't they?"

"Yes, they are," I conceded.

His simple and direct response had the exact effect on me he had hoped for. I was beginning to feel like a bit of a whiner, as I thought about the nice lifestyle I had been enjoying for years and the generous rewards I had received at work. His point well taken, he knew I was now open to hearing more.

I'll get back to this lunch story, but I want to paint a bigger picture of my Dad's effect on people, through me.

I still have the notes from that lunch that my assistant typed up and that I shared with my coworkers afterward. They were feeling as down as I was at the time.

During the years, my Dad had grown famous among my peers. In many ways, he had become the motivator for us all. If we were going through a bad time, it was not unusual, for example, for Chip to stand up in the middle of the room and ask, "What would your Dad say about this one, Mary?" Chip, one of my favorite people at the company, kept typed-up notes from my Dad lunches on his bulletin board.

At meetings, my peers would often wonder out loud, "What would Mary's Dad have to say about that?" He was so helpful at reminding us what was good in any bad situation we might be in.

It wasn't just my work friends that he counseled. The title I chose for this book *Lunch Meat and Life Lessons* actually came from my niece Mandy who, when she was down or lonely, would say, "I need to go spend some time with Grandpa and get some lunch meat and life lessons, and I know I will feel better."

Perhaps it's time to gather another lesson.

BUTCHER'S WISDOM

Look for the good news to balance the bad.
They're still paying you aren't they?

CHAPTER ELEVEN:

Meet the Challenge

WE WERE STILL SEATED AT THE BAR, almost finished with lunch. My Dad signaled for another German beer and asked me if I wanted anything more. I shook my head.

"What I do want to know, Dad, is how to deal with the negatives at work. I'm not the only one having a hard time with the new regime."

"First thing I am going to tell you about that," he said, "is to 'meet the challenge.'"

BUTCHER'S WISDOM

Deal with it. Meet the challenge.

"Meet the challenge?" I whined.

I felt less guilty about whining as I thought he was actually sounding a bit too preachy for my appetite just then. He sensed my impatience and just smiled at me. How he ever accumulated all the patience he showed I will never know.

I have often tried to figure out what Dad was for me in

these encounters. He wasn't really a teacher, since he wasn't just handing out facts and information. Neither was he a therapist or a psychiatrist, since he wasn't primarily interested in my feelings, but in practical solutions. There was a lot of homespun philosophy in his wisdom, but he wasn't really a philosopher, though that was the description—"city philosopher"—the newspaper gave him in his obituary. I think the nearest thing Dad was to me was a professional coach. Not a rah-rah kind of sports coach, but the kind of coach professional people go to for no-nonsense clarity and direction in their personal lives and careers.

"Yes," he said, "Meet the challenge. I think that's exactly how you should look at bad times—as a series of challenges to be met. Not won or lost, but met."

"You are suggesting I deal with this situation as if I were meeting a challenge?"

"If you can say 'I met the challenge' on the other side of a bad situation, that means you came out of it feeling good about yourself. Besides, the only thing you can ever really control in any situation you don't have control over is how you feel about how you dealt with it, right?"

"Right," I replied. I probably still sounded a little incredulous, but I found myself thinking about how correct he was.

"Is this helping?" he asked.

"You know it is, Dad," I responded honestly.

I did get his points but I still wasn't feeling very optimistic and I'm sure it showed.

However, I noticed that the bartender, even though he looked busy, was totally focused on my Dad and the wisdom he was pouring out for me with all the intensity of his heart. The bartender recognized the truth that was coming out of his mouth and didn't want to miss a word.

"Mary, I know the situation you are in now is not the one

you want to be in, but it is what it is. However it ends up is yet to be determined, but how you manage your way though it will determine how you feel about it on the other side."

"The other side?" I said.

"Trust me, there will be another side." he said.

I remained silent, so he went on.

"One thing you can always count on is that the highs and lows will come and go. Once you realize that, I think you will have a lot more fun along the way, and you will lighten up some. Which brings me to my next piece of advice: Stop taking it all so seriously! Have you ever heard the saying, 'Don't take life too seriously, you are never going to get out of it alive anyway'?"

BUTCHER'S WISDOM

Don't take life too seriously.
You are never going to get out of it alive anyway.

Yes," I smiled. "Many times. From you. But I do feel lately a little like not much is going right— like I lost all my good luck."

"Good luck? Bad luck? Who knows?" he replied.

"What does that mean?" I asked.

"Good luck? Bad luck? Who knows?" he repeated. "It means exactly that. Don't get so down about this string of events, because you don't know where it will go or where it will take you. Maybe what you think is bad luck is really good luck? Who knows? These changes in your work world may be the best thing that ever happened to you. You may very well end up in an even better place, if you handle it correctly," he nodded.

"Maybe," I said a little doubtfully. "Who knows?

"Let me tell you about a time when there was a huge change in my life. It was on July 13, 1951. The meat market had been doing very well and things were moving along quite nicely for my business, kind of like your career up to now. And then every thing turned upside down when the big flood wiped out my business entirely."

The bartender gave up any pretense of being busy. He came over and stood right next to us, listening intently.

"Even with all the reports and the evacuation plans," my Dad continued, "I really didn't believe there would be a flood, until it actually happened. It was the middle of the night when your mother ran into the bedroom and woke me up screaming, 'John! John! Wake up! It's over the L! It's over the L!'"

"It's over the L?" I asked. "What in the world does that mean?"

"The flood." he replied. "You know, up the hill from the meat market where the Milgram's Grocery store is, there's that big vertical sign that reads M-I-L-G-R-A-M-S from top to bottom? She was screaming 'It's over the L!' because the water was over the L in Milgrams."

"Wow," I replied. If the flood had covered Milgrams, it had certainly covered Dad's meat market.

"I got out of bed and went into the living room. When I looked at the television pictures of the rising flood waters, and saw the M-I and no L-G-R-A-M-S, I felt sick. I don't need to tell you what was happening to the meat market when the store up the hill was under water."

"What did you do?" my eyes widened in suspense.

"I thought a minute about what I might do, and then told your mother to turn off the television set and come back to bed. She looked at me like I was crazy. 'But John, the water is over the L!' she kept saying."

"'Exactly,' I told her. 'The water is over the L and there is nothing I can do about it. Now come back to bed and let's enjoy the fact that we can sleep late for a change.'"

He smiled and seemed to get carried away in memory for a moment, a memory that could have, and probably should have been a bad one. And yet, I could tell he did not look at it that way. This was obviously a fond memory for him, and at that moment I think we were both missing Mom.

"'Over the L,'" I repeated. "Your entire work world is under water and all you can think about is that you got to sleep in for once in your life?"

"No," he replied. "That's what I *chose* to think about at that moment. There's a big difference," he said. "And maybe you should do the same. All those people above you at work, coming and going, doing things you may not agree with, you can't control any of those things anymore than I could control the flood waters."

BUTCHER'S WISDOM

Some things are just "over the L."

"Sometimes, you have to resign yourself to the fact that some things are just 'over the L,'" he told me.

"Okay," I nodded and smiled at him. "I will."

"Good," he said. "And you know that saying 'Good luck?

Bad luck? Who knows?' is so true. You never know what will come out of bad times."

Dad went on to explain that there were actually a lot of really good things that came out of the '51 flood.

"I can tell you that as devastating as it was at the moment," he said, "we would not be where we are today, financially, had it not been for that disaster."

"Why's that?" I asked.

"Because of the flood, I was offered a chance to borrow money at a 3 percent interest rate. I had no intentions of doing that as I had saved enough over the years to rebuild the market myself, but a very wise friend told me to borrow all I could and to invest it in real estate. Well, I did. And I made some very wise decisions as to properties to buy. That started a whole new income stream for our family that I never would have realized if it wasn't for the flood. That's why I firmly believe in the saying 'Good luck? Bad luck? Who knows?'"

"I got it Dad," I said. And I meant it.

BUTCHER'S WISDOM

Good luck? Bad luck? Who knows?

I felt so much better about everything and most of all, I just felt loved. I think that's when I realized more than ever before what our lunches together were all about.

Yes, I cherished the advice and wisdom he gave me but, most of all, I just cherished the time with him and the feeling

I always walked away with after being in his presence.

Good times, bad times and all the times in between, I could always count on him to help me put it in perspective, because I could always count on his love. And that helped me put it in perspective the most!

I was blessed and I knew it.

Chapter Twelve:

Prepare Yourself

THEY SAY BAD THINGS HAPPEN IN THREES. I am not sure who "they" are or how "they" know that, but that saying certainly held true for me in 2004.

The workplace concerns that had taken center stage in my world seemed insignificant, as I was forced to deal with three losses that would forever change my world. I had no idea that the last lesson my father would teach me was that I should take the principle of "put it in perspective" and actually put it in perspective.

As the year began I was verging on being so wrapped up in myself that I was in jeopardy of becoming a damn small package.

My company continued to move in a direction I was not all that happy with, and I had just been informed that I was going to have yet another new boss. Frankly, I anticipated this as a welcome change, that is, until he arrived and I saw his effect on others. He lacked both patience and people skills, which led to the steady departure of many remaining colleagues whom I had respected and admired most. The exodus continued as others made the decision to leave the company.

In spite of the change in leadership, I was doing really well most of the time. In fact, I was doing some of my best work and I continued to be well rewarded for it. However, with this new boss and a new influx of negative energy swirling around me, I was again finding it increasingly difficult to stay focused and to keep my blinders on.

As a result, I continued to rely on lunches with Dad to help keep me motivated and put things in perspective. One day, when I was particularly conflicted about the way my new boss handled a conversation with one of my coworkers, I drove over to Dad's house. I phoned him to say I was coming. It had been raining most of the morning, and still was, so I drove right up to the back door.

Dad was waiting for me on the side porch, as I closed my umbrella and opened the door. We exchanged kisses.

Before I knew it, I started telling him about the horrible way my new boss was treating Stan.

"I know that the new boss likes my work and my approval rating is up to the roof with him," I added, "but I can't stand the way he treats others, Dad. What can I do?"

Dad tried to calm me down.

"I am happy to hear that you are doing some great work and that this boss of yours is good to you," he said. "As far as what to do, come on over to the butcher block and we'll have a chat."

He had lunch already cooking on the griddle. I could smell it. He knew how much I loved his pork chops and fried potatoes.

It was already approaching fall, so I noticed Dad's straw hat hanging on the hook by the door in the kitchen, his leather cap now on his head. As he grew older, his everyday outfit consisted of a pair of pants, without a belt, held up by suspenders. He still wore his neatly laundered and pressed white shirts. A seamstress had replaced all the front buttons of his shirts with zippers because his hands were too big to work the buttons.

"To be honest I am not sure what you should do," he said, "but from what you say about the way he treats people and how opposite it is from the way you like to work, I wonder how long you will want to work for this guy."

He paused for a moment to think, rubbing his big right hand over his chin.

I waited quietly for him to continue.

"I wonder if maybe it might not be time to look for another limb."

"Another limb?" I asked.

"Yes" he said. "I have always believed that you don't let go of one limb until you have a firm hold on another. When the limb you are holding onto so tightly starts feeling weak, there isn't anything wrong with taking a look to see if there might be another limb out there that would be better for you to grab onto."

BUTCHER'S WISDOM

Don't let go of one limb until you have a firm hold on another.

"Are you telling me it's time to move on, Dad?" I asked.

"You know endings are inevitable and you always want to be as prepared for them as you can be," he said. "The best endings are the ones you are prepared for."

BUTCHER'S WISDOM

The best endings are the ones you are prepared for.

For the first time in nearly 25 years, I started to open myself up to the idea that maybe I could and would do something else with my career. It was after that lunch that I began to look at what other limbs there might be out there for me to grab onto. I started to take calls from recruiters whom I had previously turned away, and I mentioned my interest to some people I knew.

However, my search was put on the shelf when our family suffered our first loss of the year. After a heroic but ugly battle with breast and lung cancer, my mother-in-law, Diane Lucas, died on August 22, 2004.

Shortly thereafter, I got a call from my Dad, who informed me that my oldest sister Joan was in the hospital. That was the start of the second loss. When doctors gave her about three months to live, Joan insisted that we move her from the hospital directly to an assisted living facility where she could spend her remaining months.

The next few months are a blur. While I managed to stay committed to my work and my boys, I wanted very much to make time for frequent visits with my sister.

In looking for the "good" in this situation, I found myself reconnecting with extended family members at a deeper level than ever before, as we all rallied together in support of Joan—and each other. With the doctors, hopeless conversations were all we seemed to have.

Dad appeared to be having trouble accepting the inevitable, that Joan was going to die. "It's not good," Dad said. "It's cancer of the throat. But I think she will pull out of it. I think she will be fine."

And then one day, everything changed. I'm not sure exactly what happened or why he finally got it, but when he did get it, I guess you could say it got him.

Although Joan was growing visibly weaker by the day, my father insisted that we all gather together to have Thanksgiving at the family home where we all grew up. We had not gathered together in that house since my mom's passing. But he was determined that, this year, we should all come back home and be together because he said, "Joan will want that."

Although we all had our doubts that she would be able to be there since she could hardly move, when Thanksgiving Day arrived, Joan was there. We were all surprised and pleased. She actually seemed more animated and alive than she had in days. She stayed almost two hours and sat at the table while we had dinner. It was obvious to all of us, including Dad, that by the time we said our good-byes, she was exhausted. As it turned out, she never did get out of bed on her own again after that day.

Maybe it was his seeing Joan so exhausted the day after Thanksgiving, or maybe it was the "Do not resuscitate" order that she signed that next day in the assisted living facility, but we all noticed a change in Dad.

During one visit to his house just after Thanksgiving, I found a letter addressed to our cousins in Germany that he was planning to send with their Christmas package. It was dated December 4, 2004:

"My health is still good. I have aches and pains but at 88 years old I feel very blessed. My wife has been gone 4 years now. My children are very good to me. I have sad news. My oldest daughter Joan has cancer of the throat, very bad. She cannot swallow food so they put a feeding tube in. The doctors say she cannot live very long. She is such a fine daughter. I will sure miss her."

It was then that I knew he had given up hope for Joan. Although he still took the eternal optimist outlook in all our conversations, they started to take on a more resigned and reflective tone.

"I've lived a good life," he would say more often than usual. "I have been blessed," was now standard in every talk, and he also started reminding me more often than usual how blessed I was to have the gift of family.

"The greatest gift your mother and I have given you is each other," he would remind me as we would leave a visit with Joan. "It is such a gift that Joan has been given, that I have been given, of this incredible supporting cast we have that is made up of our family."

I could sense something was not the same, but I just thought that this was his version of sad. None of us were our usual selves during that period, but how could we be? It was all just so heartbreaking.

I was soon to find out, however, that, for Dad, it was more than his version of sad; it was his decision of what I believe to be timing. As he watched our round-the-clock vigils begin at Joan's bedside, I think he just decided that he wanted this to be his time too.

On December 12th, in Dad's typical "I-don't-want-to-bother-any-of-you-kids-and-interrupt-your-busy-lives" fashion, he drove himself to the emergency room complaining of pains in his chest. He stayed three days, declining all suggestions of any type of surgery that could help his failing heart. Three days was just enough time to get his strength back so that he could go home and "get his house in order" as he insisted he must do.

He was released on the 15th and would not let anyone stay with him; nor would he consider staying anywhere else. He went straight home and straight to work. The piles of papers and files that had been in such disarray after my Mom's passing were organized and laid out in a way that Jim, my oldest living brother and the executor of Dad's estate, would know where everything was when he needed to find it. There were envelopes marked with each one of our names, and he even talked openly as to what we should do about his funeral. Always the bargain hunter, he wondered if there was such a thing as "two for the price of one" funeral.

On the fourth day, when the heartache was too much to bear and he was too weak to drive himself back to the hospital, he called an ambulance. I felt like I was in a dream. I had just left Joan's bedside when I received the call to come to the hospital for Dad.

"This can't be happening," I said out loud as I was driving to the hospital.

I had no idea when I arrived at the hospital what the next 48 hours would hold. We all knew Joan was going to die. We had spent the last three months preparing ourselves for that. We had said our good-byes, and had come to peace with her end being near. But now it looked like we were losing Dad at the same time, and it was something I just couldn't fathom.

Visiting him at the hospital, I was surprised to see him as animated and jovial as always. I walked in to the emergency room and he raised both palms to the air and said, "Vas Cant E do gar Nix," which was his German version of "it's over the L."

The best I can translate it is, "What can I do but nothing?"

I looked at my sister Jane standing at the bedside and her face told me everything I needed to know: it wasn't good. Dad introduced me to his nurse, explaining that she came from a family he thought a lot of and, as usual, was laying the come-back sauce on her.

I kissed him on the forehead and he said in a quiet voice, "I just want to go home."

"We know, Dad," Jane said. "But they want to take you to Intensive Care until we can get you home with hospice care.

It's Christmas week and they are doing their best to get you a bed and all you need so that you *can* go home. Right now we just have to wait."

He smiled at her and nodded his okay. His hands went back up in the air, palms raised to the heavens as he once again said, "Vas Cant E do gar Nix."

Everyone did what needed to be done to get Dad home and somehow still manage to spend time with Joan.

As we settled Dad in his room in intensive care and signed all the papers so that he could go peacefully when he was ready, he asked that all the wires and tubes be removed and the monitors be turned off as he wanted to "rest in peace" while we waited. I sat in a chair across from his bed and for a while we sat in silence, which was unusual for the two of us.

"You need anything?" I asked.

"You," he responded. "You're too far away and you look uncomfortable. Why don't you climb up here in this bed and lay next to me. Nobody will care. Put your head right here," he said as he touched the crook of his arm.

And so I did.

He must have felt my tears on his shoulder as I laid my head down because he said, "Are you okay?"

I thought for a moment, wondering how I could possibly respond to that question.

"No," I said. "I'm not okay. I was prepared for Joan to be leaving us, but this, this I am not prepared for."

"Well," he sighed. "I am ready. I've lived a good life. I like what I see in the mirror when I wake up every morning. I am proud of who I am, what I have done and what I am leaving behind. I have lived a life preparing for this and if this is the way it ends, then this is the way it ends. I'm ready."

"But Dad, who will I have lunch with? Who will inspire me from now on?" I asked.

"You don't need me to inspire you. You don't need someone else to complete you. Inspire yourself," he said. "Your mother and I taught you well, remember what you have learned and inspire yourself."

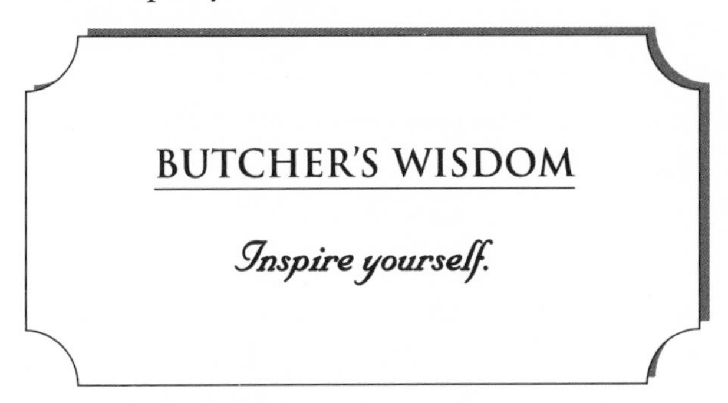

He paused for a moment to get his breath.

"You will find the next limb to grab on to and you will be just fine without me. Now, let's close our eyes and rest while we wait." Then, he added with a grin I will never forget, "I want to have enough strength to make you a big steak on the grill when I get home."

As he grew weaker and the wait grew longer, "I will cook you a steak" turned into "Will you cook a steak for me?" and by the time the ambulance came to take him back to his home, it had become "Will someone go out and pick up a steak for me at Applebee's?"

And so my brother Jerry did.

Dad got home in time to have his steak, open his Christmas cards, listen to his phone messages and say goodnight to his children, grandchildren and great-grandchildren. Then, he fell asleep in his home in front of the fireplace. He never woke up. In the end, he died peacefully the morning of December 21st.

After he was gone, we went to see Joan and tell her that she could "go now." We told her that Dad was gone and that she could go in peace, and that he was waiting for her along with Mom and her husband Lou and all those in our family who had gone before her. She passed away at 12:01 a.m. on December 22nd.

Over the next five days, we "carried on" in a fog, reminding ourselves of the words our parents found comfort in whenever they lost someone they loved. "Thy will be done."

We planned the funeral and found out there is such a thing as a "two for the price of one." The family reunited on the 26th for the visitation and the double funeral on the 27th.

More than a thousand people came to pay their respects and show their support for the family that both Joan and Dad had loved so much. When the funeral was over, we all went back to our lives, because that is what we had to do.

As for me, I buried myself in work. I was asked countless times by caring coworkers if I needed more time, but I just wanted to get back at it, to bury myself in it.

Over the next five months, I forgot about looking for another limb and accepted the additional responsibilities a recent promotion had created for me. I was recognized and rewarded for what I accomplished in my new role. I was hoping that it would help me remember what it felt like to be in the midst of the happiness of pursuit. Truth be told, it just wasn't there for me there anymore. I needed a change in order to feel fully alive again, but I wasn't sure what that change looked like.

"I can't just quit, can I?" I asked a friend. "Dad told me you don't let go of one limb without having a firm hold on another."

"I think it is all in how you define the limb," my friend said. "Because your Dad died a wealthy man, emotionally and financially, you have been blessed. Not only did he give you the wisdom to help you make it to where you are, but also to succeed where you're going. He has afforded you the opportunity, if you want, to climb down from the tree where you are and feel the grass at your feet for a while. Take a well-deserved break and then you will figure out the next tree you want to climb, in due time, thanks to him."

I thanked my friend for the good advice. He helped me 'put it in perspective.' I thought about my situation all evening.

The next day at work, I resigned. I left my company at the top of my game as they say, and I have never looked back.

As I spent that first summer enjoying the grass under my feet, following my boys from one sporting event to the next, I thought about what my next limb might look like and I thought often about my father and what an inspiration he was to me, especially in the end.

There were just so many lessons he taught me that I did not want to let any of them get lost or forgotten. So, I decided that in order *to inspire myself* as he suggested, I needed to be more of an inspiration *for* myself. Although I was proud of my past career success, I was ready to get my house in order so that on my last day I would honestly be able to say all the things Dad said on his last day:

"I like what I see in the mirror when I wake up every morning. I am proud of who I am, what I have done and what I am leaving behind. I have lived a life preparing for this, and if this is the way it ends, then this is the way it ends. I'm ready."

I decided to do something that I would be proud of and that I knew both my father and mother would be proud of me for doing. I decided to write this book. In order to help me get inspired again and to help others inspire themselves. I decided to share the legacy and lessons I was so blessed to have been exposed to because I was—no, because I am and always will be the Butcher's Daughter.

"To live in hearts we leave behind is not to die."

John Bichelmeyer, 88 years old, 2004
Photographer Daughter Joan Grimm

EPILOGUE

ALTHOUGH SOME TIME HAS PASSED NOW since Dad's death, there is still not a day that goes by when I don't say a silent prayer of gratitude for the blessing of his wisdom.

I am still working at sharing his wisdom. Now, as president of my own consulting firm, I work daily at trying to be the kind of coach for others that my father was for me.

I am also still working daily at being the kind of person who can say on my last day, all the things my Dad was able to say on his last day.

I am still stunned at how he orchestrated his passing.

One of the only times I ever saw him uncertain and sad was the day of my brother's funeral. It was December 24th, 1965. I was 7 years old at the time, and my brother Johnny was 21.

Johnny had graduated from college in May of that year and had moved to Colorado where he was working on a ranch and as a disc jockey at a local radio station. We had not expected to have him home that year for the holidays, but Johnny had different plans. He called Dad and said, "I'll be home for Christmas," and told him not to tell anyone because he wanted to surprise Mom.

About ten miles from home, he fell asleep at the wheel and his car hit a concrete pillar. He died in the early morning hours of December 23rd, and we buried him the next day, Christmas Eve.

Most of that day and those that followed, I watched Dad deal with this blow exactly as he dealt with every other loss—with strength, dignity and acceptance.

There was one brief moment, however, that I witnessed when the pain, sorrow and grief overwhelmed him. It was just after the casket was closed at the funeral home, where he watched my Mom struggle with letting Johnny go. He had comforted her and guided her to the car that would take us to the church for the funeral and was strong for her until the door closed and the driver pulled away.

In the car at the time it was just Mom, Dad, the driver and us "little girls," Jeannie, Jane, me, and Barbie. As the car drove off to follow the hearse, Mom pulled herself together, wanting to be strong in front of us, I am sure, and it was then that Dad put his head in his big hands and just sobbed.

He cried all the way to the church, his grief overwhelming him. We all sat quietly watching him, completely awestruck and heartbroken ourselves. I think I was in awe because here was this man I had never seen vulnerable before, so hurt and broken. My heart ached, not only because of the loss of my brother, but also because of the effect of this loss on my parents.

When we arrived at the church, he pulled himself together and lifted his head. "Thy will be done," he whispered and we all got out of the car and went in to the funeral.

From that moment on, he was the pillar of strength and, as usual, he was an example for all of us as to how to respond to the most tragic events that life deals you.

I continue to be inspired not only by the way he lived his life but the way he left this life, prepared and on his terms—and before he would bear the heartache of another lost child.

I find it ironic that we remember Dad's passing on the 21st of December; Joan, his oldest daughter on the 22nd; and Johnny, his oldest son, on the 23rd.

I think "Thy will be done" is God's version of "It's over the L."

Mom and Dad chose "Thy will be done" as the epitaph for Johnny.

"To live in hearts we leave behind is not to die" is the epitaph that we chose for Mom and Dad.

BUTCHER'S LEGACY*

To live in hearts we leave behind is not to die.

**A portion of any proceeds realized as a result of the publication of this book will be donated to the American Heart Association in memory of John and Mary Bichelmeyer.*

"The first hunk of meat you sell is yourself."

John Bichelmeyer, the Butcher, circa 1955

Photographer Unknown

A Special Note to Readers:

If you've come this far in *Lunchmeat & Life Lessons*, chances are you like what you're reading—and learning—from the smartest man I ever knew. In fact, maybe by coming this far in the book you feel as if you know him, too.

To help keep The Butcher's Wisdom alive in your daily life, I've summarized all of the gems presented in this book over the next few pages. You may find it helpful to reference these from time to time, clip them out as reminders to add to your daily planner or dashboard, maybe even tape to the fridge.

However and wherever you use The Butcher's Wisdom, I am certain that these life lessons can and will enrich your life.

A Butcher's Wisdom Tear Out Summary

In the Beginning

Show 'em what you're made of!
The first hunk of meat you sell is yourself.

Create a Lasting Impression

Remember the comeback sauce.

Stay Focused

Get out your blinders and put them on.

Make Something Happen

Don't be a waver–do be a doer.
Be on time all the time.
Be a person who makes something happen.

Bring out the Best

If you don't like someone than they don't like you.
You've gotta find the like.

Admit Your Mistakes

Raise your hand, put it down and get back to playing the game.

Enjoy the Ride

Learn something from every person you meet.

It's not the pursuit of happiness, but the happiness of pursuit that inspires.

Stay busy. Idle time is the devils workshop.

Don't act like it's your due—take every chance to say thank you.

When you're all wrapped up in yourself you make a damn small package.

Nobody can make you happy but yourself.

Look for Happiness Within

The happiest people are the ones who are inspired and enjoying the ride they are on while they are on it.

Celebrate Life

Celebrate every chance you get.

Send yourself flowers.

Put Bad Things in Perspective

Look for the good to balance the bad.
They're still paying you aren't they?

Meet the Challenge

Deal with it–meet the challenge.
Don't take life too seriously–you are never going to get out of it alive anyway.
Some things are just "Over the L."
Good luck? Bad luck? Who knows?

Prepare Yourself

Don't let go of one limb till you have a firm hold on another.
The best endings are the ones you are prepared for.
Inspire yourself.

Epilogue

To live in hearts we leave behind is not to die.

COMEBACK SAUCE

LUNCHMEAT & LIFE LESSONS

Sharing a Butcher's Wisdom

Now for my own **COMEBACK SAUCE...**

As I mention in Chapter 2, the recipe for comeback sauce can be as simple as just saying "thank you."

So that is exactly what I want to do—I want to thank you for reading my book.

I also want to thank you for helping me to keep my father's legacy alive by using and passing on his wisdom in your own lives, both personal and professional.

I invite you to share with me any questions, comments or thoughts about the book by contacting me at:

MBL Consulting, LLC
7301 Mission Road
Suite 328A
Prairie Village, KS 66208
(913) 671-7974

Email: mary@consultwithmbl.com

Web site: www.consultwithmbl.com

I look forward to hearing your own stories of how you applied the **Butcher's Wisdom!**

"The greatest gift we leave you is each other!"

Bichelmeyer family photo, circa 1967

Mary seated on her fathers lap